Sebastian Painadath sj

The Power of Silence

Sebastian Painadath sj

The Power of Silence

50 Meditations to Discover
the Divine Space within you

2011

The Power of Silence: *Fifty Meditations to Discover the Divine Space Within You*— Published by the Rev. Dr. Ashish Amos of the Indian Society for Promoting Christian Knowledge (ISPCK), Post Box 1585, 1654, Madarsa Road, Kashmere Gate, Delhi-110006.

© S. Painadath, SJ, 2009

Revised Edition, 2011

Meditation diagrams: Roy M. Thottam sj
Suryanamaskar postures: Devassy Mookanur

All rights reserved. No part of this book may be reproduced or transmitted in any form or by any means, electronic, mechanical, photocopying, recording, or by any information storage and retrieval system, without the prior permission in writing from the publisher.

The views expressed in the book are those of the author and the publisher takes no responsibility for any of the statements.

ISBN: 978-81-8465-169-0

Laser typeset by **ISPCK,** Post Box, 1585, 1654, Madarsa Road, Kashmere Gate, Delhi-110006.
Tel: 23866323/22
e-mail– ashish@ispck.org.in • ella@ispck.org.in
website-www.ispck.org.in

Contents

How to use this Handbook 10

Part I. Way to Silence

1.	**The Body**	**26**
1.1.	Accept oneself	28
1.2.	Sit earthed	30
1.3.	Sit rooted	32
1.4.	Be in the body	34
1.5	Feel through the body	36
2.	**The Breath**	**38**
2.1	Feel the breath	40
2.2.	Feel the stream of breath	42
2.3.	Feel the energy centres	44
2.4.	The body in becoming	46
2.5.	In harmony with all	48
3.	**The Word**	**50**
3.1.	The key word	52
3.2.	The divine name	54
3.3.	The mantra OM	56
3.4.	The cosmic tone	58
3.5.	The eternal now	60

Part II. Symbols of Silence

4.	**The Fountain**	**64**
4.1.	The way to the depth	66
4.2.	The Father as the hidden spring	68
4.3.	The Son as the well	70
4.4.	The Spirit as the flow	72
4.5.	We are the channels	74
5.	**The Tree**	**76**
5.1	The Father as the hidden root	78
5.2.	The Son as the stem	80
5.3.	The Spirit as the vital sap	82
5.4.	We are branches in the Divine	84
5.5.	We are branches of one another	86
6.	**The New Life**	**88**
6.1.	Life in flesh	90
6.2.	God in flesh	92
6.3.	Life in Christ	94
6.4.	Life in the Spirit	96
6.5.	The divine life	98
7.	**The Seed**	**100**
7.1.	Detachment	102
7.2.	The Ground of being	104
7.3.	The dynamic oneness	106
7.4.	Birth of God in the soul	108
7.5.	Universal theophany	110
8.	**The Master**	**112**
8.1.	The surrender	114
8.2.	The indwelling	116
8.3.	The oneness	118
8.4.	The cosmic vision	120
8.5.	The solidarity	122

Part III. Graces of Silence

9.	**The Way**	**126**
9.1.	The human suffering	128
9.2.	The divine suffering	130
9.3.	The healing presence	132
9.4.	The divinisation	134
9.5.	The new creation	136
10.	**The Now**	**138**
10.1	Inner freedom	140
10.2.	Confidence	142
10.3.	Transparency	144
10.4.	Attentiveness	146
10.5.	Compassion	148

Silence Empowers Us 150

Appendix: Body as the Language of Prayer 152
    A Meditative Form of Sūryanamaskar (Sun Salutation)

*Go to the inner silent space;
    meet the Divine therein*

Gospel according to Mathew, 6:6.

*Seek the Divine within
    the silent space in you*

Chandogya Upanishad, 8:11.

How to use this Handbook

Search for the Divine

This handbook of meditation took shape in the course of three decades. From 1978 onwards I have been giving series of retreats and meditation courses in India, Europe and in the East Asian countries. My experiences with them and the responses of the participants have contributed much to the formation of this handbook. Thus it is a book that has evolved out of lived praxis. I gratefully remember the hundreds of seekers who have journeyed with me on the spiritual pilgrimage.

I have noticed four problems which Christian spiritual seekers encounter worldwide. They say:

- I cannot pray because I am unable to sit in inner silence and concentration.
- I enjoy remaining in silent meditation without an object, but God has disappeared from my spiritual horizons.
- I can focus attention on the Divine, but I do not meet Christ on my inner journey.
- I relish meditation, but I cannot relate it with the activities of my daily life.

Basically the problem is with regard to the experience of the personal God: how far is the divine reality to be understood as personal, and how to enter into an inter-personal relation with God? Christian tradition emphasises the personal character of the Divine in the light of God's self-revelation in Jesus Christ. But believers often get stuck in the primal forms of a personified image of God and get settled in elementary forms of devotion to an anthropomorphic God; or else, they experience no access to a personal God at all and hence find it almost impossible to pray. We need to look at this phenomenon in the global spiritual context.

Awaken the Mystic

We live in a new age of the spiritual evolution of humanity. It is characterised by the global process of inter-religious encounter. Religions which were for centuries considered far-off realities come closer to one another through inter-cultural communication and inter-continental encounter. Today no religion is in fact totally alien to anyone. The major Scriptures are translated into world languages, the religious symbols impress on people beyond barriers and spiritual masters speak to the hearts of seekers everywhere. Followers of different religions give witness to their deep inter-dependence through dialogue and collaboration. A *mystical wind* is blowing across the globe: the diversity of religions is respected and the converging lines in spirituality are recognised. Believers are becoming critical of the traditional language of theology and symbols of rituals. They are looking for a genuine access to a mystical experience of the Divine. This search often takes them beyond the boundaries of their traditional religiosity and leads them to the well-springs of other religions. Those who get panicked by this movement of the divine Spirit react through restorative directives or fundamentalist patterns of thought and action.

In this global movement of the *Spirit that blows where it wills*, each religion has to reflect on the meaning and message of its foundational experience. In this context we Christians have to meet Christ anew. We need to ask: what is the Spirit telling the Church today? (Rev. 3, 29). If a growing number of Christian seekers finds it difficult to relate to a God that is presented in the traditional personified forms and anthropomorphic images, one has to ask what this crisis of faith really means. Perhaps this *sign of the times* is an invitation to carve deeper and awaken the mystic in the Church. Mystics have been persistently asking believers to go beyond *names and forms* towards the incomprehensible mystery of the Divine. The caution of Augustine is here in place: "If you know God, it is not God!".

Meeting Christ

In this book I am pursuing this question. The spiritual aspirations and agonies of hundreds of Christian seekers, with whom I journeyed in three decades, form the living context of my search. A basic question that they ask is this: where and how do we experience Christ? In the mainstream tradition of the Church we experience him as:

- Jesus of history, whom one recalls from the past
- Christ of faith, whom one encounters in the present
- Christ the King, who is extolled at the *right hand* of the Father in the heavens
- Christ the Lord, whom one adores in the Blessed Sacrament

- Christ the Master, whom one follows in daily life
- Christ the Liberator, who one meets in the poor
- Christ the Saviour, whom one proclaims as the *only* way at variance with other saviour-figures.

These are vital elements of Christian faith; in them there is an emphasis on the personified form, which invites a devotional surrender to Christ, the divine *thou*. Inevitably psychological elements and sociological factors shape the devotional forms of faith in Christ. However Christian mystics call for a deeper awareness of the presence of Christ within the human heart and in the spiritual evolution of the world. They emphasise the trans-personal dimension of the presence of Christ: Christ is the divine *I*.

- Christ is God-in-us here and now
- Christ is God-with-us in the present
- Christ is the unfolding of the Divine in the human and the transparency of the human to the Divine
- Christ is the unity of the Divine and the human
- Christ is the compassionate God who suffers with us and transforms our life into the new life
- Christ is the power of God in the universal process of salvation in which other religions are integrated.

The transition from an inter-personal relationship (*bhakti*) to a trans-personal consciousness (*jñāna*), from an encounter with Christ as the divine *thou* before us to the experience of Christ as the divine *self* within us, from a devotional surrender to the person of Jesus to a mystical awareness of the divine presence of Christ, from a dichotomisation of the divine and the human dimensions in Christ to a perception of the hypostatic oneness of the two, is the running theme of this book. I do not want to claim that with this transition all questions are answered, but I do feel that by awakening the mystical dimension of Christic spirituality the Church could address the spiritual search of many Christians, who find themselves on the border-lines of the traditional patterns of theology and spirituality. With this I do not devalue the role of devotional forms of faith in Christ expressed in popular religiosity, but I want to emphasise that these need to be refined by the orientation that Jesus himself gave: *worship God in Spirit and Truth* (Jn. 4, 24)

The Inner Journey

What I intend to offer in this book is not so much a systematic theological reflection, rather exercises for a spiritual process. The main concerns are:

- To get in touch with oneself at a deeper level
- To perceive the inner dynamics of one's psyche
- To discern the movements of the divine Spirit in the inner sacred space
- To respond to the invitation of the Spirit: feel into the *depth of the Divine*
- To experience the power of Christ in the present
- To experience the presence of the risen Christ
- To perceive our life evolving *within* the Trinitarian process of life
- To seek the wider horizons of the movements of the Spirit in the world
- To listen to what the Spirit is telling us through the Scriptures and symbols of other religions.

Concrete meditation exercises are offered to pursue the inner spiritual process. Some psychological helps are proposed to get in touch with oneself at a deeper level. Certain methods of concentration are offered to help the seeker enter into a deep silence. The experiences of several spiritual masters of Christian and Indian heritage are brought in for guidance on the inward journey. The entire journey evolves in a process of contemplative silence:

- One is helped here to feel a bodily silence
- In the silence one accepts oneself as one is and has become
- It is a silence that makes one listen to the divine Word within
- In this silence one is made alert to the movements of the divine Spirit within and all around
- It is a silence in which one attunes oneself to the grace of Christ-consciousness within oneself.
- In this contemplative silence one experiences the Divine as the ultimate *subject* of one's being
- In this silence one is made sensitive to the Divine as manifested in the diversity of religions and in the secular culture.

Levels of Consciousness

The inner spiritual journey in contemplative silence takes the seeker (*sādhaka*) through three levels of consciousness: the mental, the psychic and the spiritual:

1. **The mental level:** This is the surface level wherein thoughts and feelings evolve. Here the mind controls all encounters with persons and things. The mind objectifies everything for it operates in the subject-object structure. At the centre of this level emerges the *I* consciousness. All that we conceive about the Divine and express through religious symbols and rituals are at this level of the mind. This is the limitation of our language in expressing our relationship with the Divine.

2. **The psychic level:** The actions and reactions at the mental level are constantly controlled by sub-conscious factors. These are shaped by one's own biography with all the repressed feelings and unexpressed thoughts; there are also elements of the collective psyche with the inherent remnants of the evolutionary process of humanity. Some of them are dramatically articulated in myths and legends. Disturbing memories and distracting thoughts from the psychic level may come up during the inner journey. Spiritual masters propose methods of dealing with them; some of these are offered in this book.

3. **The spiritual level:** Deep within us there is a faculty of introspection: the *buddhi*. It is like the inner light, the inner eye. All spiritual masters speak of this faculty of intuitive perception (*nous*). When this inner light is kindled, when this inner eye is opened, one looks into the *sacred space* within. This is the divine abode, the inner temple, the cave of the heart, the garden of the soul. Referring to this Jesus said: when you pray, first go into your inner room (*tamieion*), close the door and therein meet God (Mt 6:6). Here one experiences one's true self (*ātman*) and the divine SELF (*Ātman*). The relation between these two is the basic question of mystical experience.

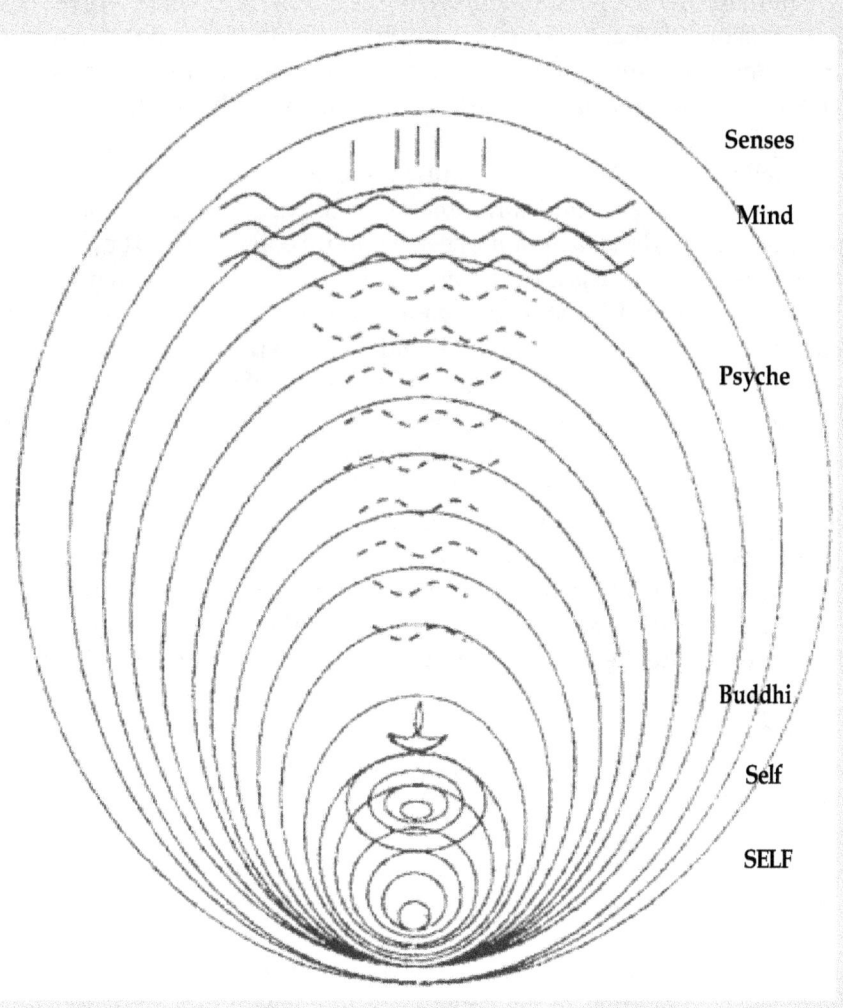

Prayer – Meditation – Contemplation

Prayer evolves expressly at the mental level. Meditation is the way to the inner faculty of the *buddhi*. Contemplation is the intuitive perception of the Divine within the inner sacred space.

In prayer an I-thou structure is inevitable. One encounters the Divine as a personal thou with names and forms. As personal beings we humans need a personal image of the Divine and hence prayer is a spontaneous element in spiritual process. As humans we do need forms and times of prayer, personal or communitarian. Prayer binds our hearts and transforms our attitudes. However the personified images of the Divine are to a great extent shaped by revelatory experiences and religious heritage, social context and psychic needs. The divine reality is in fact beyond all names and forms. The Indian spiritual masters demand that a genuine seeker should constantly go beyond the *saguna*-Iswara towards the *nirguna*-Brahman: from God with names and forms towards the Divine beyond names and forms. For a Christian seeker devotion to the person of Christ should lead to the exploration of 'the breadth and the length, the height and the depth of the love of Christ' so that one is 'filled with the utter fullness of God'' (Eph. 3, 18-19). Hence the Christian mystics alert the believers on the incomprehensible mystery of the Divine: the Divine is beyond *God* (Eckhart). Meditation (*meditari* = going to the divine Centre) is the process of moving from an interpersonal encounter with God to a transpersonal experience of the Divine within, from mental pursuits to intuitive perception at the level of the buddhi (*dhyāna* = *dhi* + *yāna* = journey to the bud*dhi*). Meditation is exploration into the deeper levels of consciousness. This inner journey takes the seeker inevitably through the realm of the psyche. In moments of intense divine grace one experiences the opening of the inner eye, with which one looks deep (*theorea*) into the inner divine space. This is contemplation (*con-templatio* = seeing with the mystical eye, that is often associated with the power-centre between the two eyebrows, *templum*). What one experiences in this divine space is something very personal and intimate. Here one should give space to the divine Spirit to act *directly* in the human self (Ignatius of Loyola). At times the human self would feel deeply *loved* by the divine Self, at other times it would feel itself as a *particle* of the Divine, and in still deeper moments the human may feel totally *one* with the Divine. Contemplation has to be open to all these dimensions of mystical experience. For a Christian seeker this is a mystical experience of being *in Christ*.

Paths of Meditation

This handbook is not offering methods of prayer; rather it offers several paths of meditation which lead to contemplation. The ten series of methods of meditation are meant to enter upon an inner process of transition

- from the extrovert mental pursuits to the introspective mystical perception,
- from devotional forms to contemplative experience,
- from dualistic conception to a unitive awareness,
- from an inter-personal relation to Christ to a trans-personal experience of being *in Christ*,
- from encountering God as personal object to experiencing the Divine as transpersonal *subject*,
- from meeting the divine *thou* to getting united with the divine *I*.

For this deepening of consciousness a preparatory stage (Series I-III) is proposed with the following steps:

- Sit rooted in the earth   Series I
- Feel through the body
- Become aware of the breathing   Series II
- Sense the power centres along the spinal chord
- Repeat attentively a key word or the
  name of the Lord   Series III
- Practice the repetition of the mantra OM.

With these simple but effective steps one enters into a space of deep silence within. One is thus enabled to have the experience of being fully here and now. When one feels that a certain amount of inner silence has set in, it is recommended to enter upon the process of meditation with a symbol (Series IV-VIII).

Power of Symbols

Symbols are a powerful means to bring together (*syn-ballein*) the diverse elements inherent in the mind and psyche. Symbols promote inner integration. In this handbook the following symbols are offered, which have a certain archetypal character. The meditative assimilation of each symbol is supported by a particular Sacred Scripture or spiritual **The** master:

- the Fountain   (Gospel of John)   Series IV
- the Tree   (Gospel of John, and Church Fathers)   Series V
- the New Life   (Paul´s Letters)   Series VI
- the Seed   (Meister Eckhart)   Series VII
- the Master   (Bhagavad Gita)   Series VIII

Inevitably one begins by visualising the symbol in imagination. This is a mental activity. But in the process of meditation the mind is transcended, the symbol is assimilated, ie. one identifies oneself with the symbol and feels the spiritual power inherent in it:

- sensing the divine Fountain opening up from the vital centre   Series IV
- feeling oneself as a branch of the divine Tree   Series V
- experiencing the insertion to the divine Life   Series VI
- growing through the transformation process of the Seed   Series VII
- listening to the inner voice of the divine Master.   Series VIII

Meditation with a symbol deepens the consciousness. As one enters into the deeper realms of inner silence the symbol gradually disappears. Only a deep sense of being *present to the present moment* remains. It is a deep awareness of being *in* the Divine, *one* with the Divine. This is how meditation evolves into contemplation. Here one lets one´s self be transformed by the divine Spirit. Here one is deeply inserted to divine life *in Christ*. This process of grace may ultimately lead to the experience of the *divinisation of the human* (*theosis*).

In the last two series (IX-X) the graces of meditation are mentioned. Here one dwells on the effects of the contemplative process on daily life, on one´s dealings with people and approach to things of nature.

- The Way: experiencing God on the way of our suffering and creative pursuits, the divinising grace in our life   Series IX
- The Now: dwelling on certain basic graces which evolve in our life in the Spirit   Series X

Twofold Movement

In every series of symbol-related meditations (Series IV-VIII) there is:
- a centripetal movement towards the divine Centre and a centrifugal movement towards the world,
- a delving into the inner divine space and a discovery of the world as the sacred space,
- a deep rootedness in the divine ground and an intense relatedness to all beings.
- an introspective journey in contemplation and an integrated approach to the activities of life,

With this twofold orientation every series of the five symbol-related meditations has the following constituent elements:
- accept oneself as one is and has become
- surrender oneself to Christ, the indwelling divine Master
- let become *one* with the dynamics of the inner-divine process
- let oneself be transformed by the divine Spirit
- look at the world by perceiving God in all and all in God
- commit oneself to the Spirit in bringing about the new creation

These exercises are not to be taken as techniques of reaching out to God; rather they are meant as helps to make oneself deeply sensitive to the working of the divine Spirit in oneself. We humans cannot conquer an access to God through assiduous efforts; we can only try to remove the road-blocks and make the inner path open for the Spirit to transform our life. Meditation is basically a receptive process. Contemplation is a gift of divine grace.

The Discipline

This is not a book to be read through. This is rather a handbook that invites an intense pursuit of meditation with regularity and discipline. Half an hour of daily meditation would suffice for seekers leading family life or having a profession. For those pursuing intense spiritual life – members of a consecrated Society, students of theology, priests, spiritual guides… – one hour of daily meditation is to be recommended. It is a great help to stick to the same hour of the day for the regular meditation, and if possible the same place and the same posture. With this discipline the body and mind get attuned to the inner process. Meditation is not just a matter of daily exercise, but it demands also a certain amount of asceticism and discipline with regard to food and rest, material possessions and personal relationships, time management and self-study (*swādhyāya*). All that contributes to inner freedom, which is an essential prerequisite for spiritual process. Meditation will then render a spiritual quality to daily life and a sacred motivation for all activities. Meditation helps a person to develop an abiding awareness of the divine presence and alertness to the given moment. Meditation becomes thus a way of life and not just a routine exercise confined to a few minutes.

The Structure of the Book

This handbook has three parts:
- Series I, II and III form the preparatory stage with the basic exercises which lead to the inner space of silence
- Series IV, V, VI, VII and VIII offer symbol-related meditations which are conducive to come to a deeper awareness of the Divine in us
- Series IX and X describe the dimensions and fruits of the awareness of the Divine.

Each meditation in every series is presented in two sections:
- On the left-hand side there is a reflection on the theme / symbol. The spiritual perspective is presented here with relevant texts from sacred Scriptures and spiritual sages. This is meant to a give a theological grounding for the corresponding meditation.
- On the right-hand side the practical guidelines for the exercise of meditation are offered. Here the steps are clearly indicated so that one can practise the meditation with a certain clarity. Occasionally some cross references to other exercises are given for further details.

The practical guidelines have the following elements which need to be carefully pursued, especially at the initial stage. Gradually one could discern what elements would be helpful to stay with the symbol / theme:
- **Posture:** this describes how to sit / walk. The basic perception is that the body is the temple of the divine Spirit
- **Breathing:** here some very simple methods of keeping awareness on breathing are proposed on the conviction that the breath of God breathes through us.

- **Inner image:** here a symbol or an image is proposed, first to visualise it, but soon to assimilate it by identifying oneself with the symbol / image. One awakens the symbol / image from within, and becomes it.
- **Recollection:** this describes how one could sense the inner movements of the Spirit and enter into a deeper awareness of the divine presence within; the content of the symbol / image deepens the consciousness
- **Inner word:** a word or phrase is proposed to be repeated within the inner space of silence. Repetition is a great help for consciousness to sink from mental activity to intuitive perception.

How to Pursue the Exercises

The 50 meditations offered here are integral elements of a transformative process that evolves with the grace of the divine Spirit. The overall purpose is to sense in deep silence the interior movements of the Spirit and to discern them in order to perceive with a certain clarity where the Spirit is leading the person. Meditation is basically a receptive process.

One may enter upon this process in the following way:

- The meditation exercises proposed in Series I, II and III have to be done with precision and discipline. These exercises are to be repeated many times. One may have to take several weeks to go through these preparatory exercises till a certain amount of inner contemplative silence has set in.
- Into this inner space of silence one takes in **just one symbol** of Series IV, V, VI, VII or VIII. Through an intense practice of meditation one awakens the symbol within the inner divine space and identifies oneself with it. This phase can be pursued in two ways:
    – either by taking 6-8 days off for an intense retreat with one symbol; one has to sit in meditation several hours daily.
    – or, by doing these exercises daily with one symbol in the course of several weeks; a special time has to be set aside every day for meditation.

In either case each meditation will have to be repeated a few times in order to sense the transformation process generated through the symbol.

- The last two sets of meditations in Series IX and X offer helps to relate the inner experience to daily life. Some basic dimensions of God-experience as well as certain effects of meditation are described here. They could be taken up after going through a symbol-related meditation process, or even during it as one senses an appropriate time for taking up one or the other meditation.

- It is important to make a daily review of the process by asking: How did I take the different steps of the exercise? How did I sense the power of inner silence? What have been the interior movements of the Spirit? Where is the divine Spirit guiding me? How is Christ-consciousness evolving in me? How is the inner experience related to daily life? The purpose here is not at all to evaluate the achievement, but to discern the direction in which the Spirit as the divine *subject* is moving me. It is good to write a spiritual journal in the course of this process taking note of the interior movements and even drawing with colours the images / diagrams which surface in the silence.

- It may be a help to draw with colours on a large size paper the diagram on the levels of consciousness (p. 15) and fix it before the desk. This could serve as a sort of route map on the inner journey.

After completing one round, one may, if need be, enter upon the inner process with another symbol given in Series IV, V, VI, VII or VIII. Since *living* with a symbol is a powerful means of deepening the spiritual consciousness, one shall not constantly change symbols.

This handbook of meditation is primarily meant for Christian seekers. Hence most of the scriptural passages, symbols and spiritual aphorisms are taken from Christian sources. But it could also be helpful to others, in as much as any genuine spiritual search for a mystical experience of the Divine takes one beyond the boundaries of traditional religions. The few quotations from Indian Scriptures do point to the converging lines of spirituality at the depth level of the consciousness of the Divine. The series of meditations based on the Bhagavad Gita (Series VIII) is an ample illustration that all genuine mystical experiences converge in the inner divine space.

In 2006 I brought out a book with fifty meditations in German: *Befreiung zum wahren Leben*, 50 meditative Schritte der Selbsterkenntnis, Kösel Verlag, Munich, 150 pages. The present book is not an exact

English translation of the original German version; however much of the material has been developed on the basis of my German book. I thank Kösel Verlag for granting the necessary permission for this.

I am grateful to Fr. George Gispert-Sauch SJ for carefully going through the manuscript and offering very valuable suggestions. I thank ISPCK, Delhi, for publishing this book. It is my hope that these meditations would help seekers experience the transforming power of contemplative silence.

19th November, 2008

Sebastian Painadath SJ,
Sameeksha
Centre for Indian Spirituality
Kalady, 683574, India
spainadath@gmail.com

PART I
Way to Silence

1. The Body

The first series of the basic exercises is meant to develop the correct bodily posture and the right inner attitude.

1. **The bodily posture.** Sit straight: keep the trunk of the body erect and relaxed and sit firm. The back, the neck and the head must be held straight. This will enable the smooth flow of the vital energies of pranah along the spinal cord. Eyes remain closed, or half open. The hands rest on the lap in *chinmudra* (index finger touching the thumb; this is associated with the pineal and pituitary glands in the brain) or in *sūrya mudra* (fingers of both the hands intertwined inside the palms; this helps assimilation of the sun energy), or else, laid open on the knees. Keep the legs in lotus / half-lotus posture (*padmāsana*) or bent in parallel to each other in a comfortable posture (*sukhāsana*); or else, sit in *vajrāsana* (sitting on the heels). It may be helpful to sit on a cushion or a small stool to be able to sit straight and relaxed.

2. **The inner attitude.** One accepts oneself totally as one has become. This would mean accepting oneself as a bodily being, bound with the earth and placed in a concrete context of life. It also means accepting one's biography with all its bright and dark sides without making any value judgement. *I am what I am.*

The inner spiritual journey starts with the mother earth. One sits like a tree rooted in the earth and senses the silence of the earth. Then one feels through one's body, the earth that one *is*. The experience of the basic oneness between the body and the earth renders a biological basis to the spiritual process. Meditation evolves at the heart of the cosmos.

The Exercises:
1. I enter upon the inner journey from where I now stand.
2. I sit united with the earth and with all things as well,
3. ...as a tree rooted in the earth, erect and alert.
4. I sit anchored at the centre of the body,
5. ...and feel through the entire body in joyful self-acceptance.

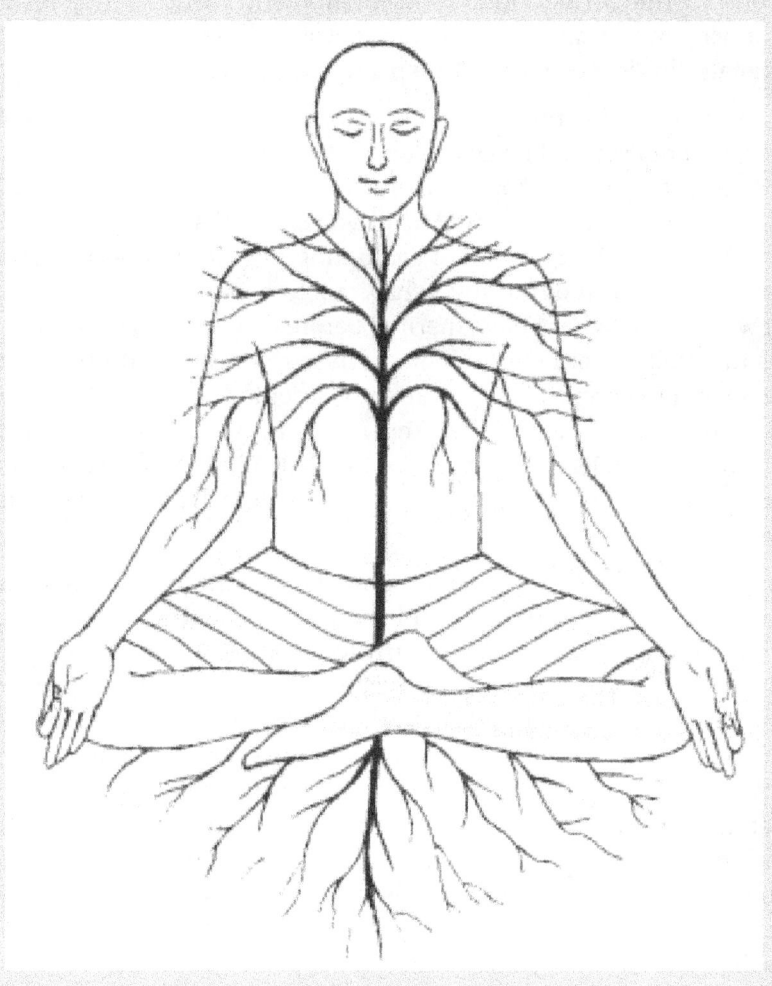

I.1. Accept Oneself

The spiritual life is like an inner pilgrimage. The longest journey that one can undertake is the journey to one's true self. When we set out on this inner journey, we grow in the ability to be present to the present moment. And as we remain alert to the present moment, we are ever *en route* on the inner journey, and always at the goal as well. The way is the already the goal – this is the grace of the spiritual journey.

Where shall I enter upon this inner spiritual pilgrimage? Exactly there, where I stand! Hence I ask myself: Where have I reached in the evolution of my life? What moves me from within? Which are the bright sides of life, and the shadows? In all honesty and seriousness I look at myself. It is a not a question of evaluating my life-process in terms of achievements or judging my behaviour to evoke guilt feelings. I do not want to ask what I have merited before God, nor do I examine my sins in detail. I just want to look at myself honestly with the divine eye. I want to accept myself as already accepted by God. I trust in the God who transforms my life. And I trust in myself because I am so precious to God. I surrender myself totally to God with the confidence that I cannot fall deeper than into his hands which always hold me in love.

From the depth of my being comes an invitation: take a new turn! I listen to this divine voice. The spiritual life demands a constant return to oneself and consequently a turn towards new directions. This is primarily a mystical movement: alertness to the Spirit that opens ever new horizons. The inner voice is related more to being than to doing, more to a deepening and broadening of consciousness than to one's achievements in life. The divine Spirit moves me to look for integral liberation that emerges from within the inner spiritual springs. The Spirit guides me to the inner divine space of freedom and love. There shines forth the Light that the Buddha experienced. Therein pours forth the stream of divine love as the Sufi mystics sensed it. There unfolds the divine spring which Jesus experienced. Into this inner *divine space* my spiritual pilgrimage takes me. From there a new way of being unfolds in my life. There I become a fountain emerging from the divine springs. Then I can bloom where I am planted.

When you pray,
go into your inner room,
close the door
and pray to the Father who is in the secret space.

Mt, 6:6

Within you
there is an inner divine space.
Seek that which is in it.
Know the Divine within you.

Chand. Up. 8.1.1

Meditation

Posture: I sit straight and relaxed. With eyes closed, I become aware of the room in which I sit: the length and breadth, the height and shape, the light and shadows, the sounds as well as the stillness. Just be here and now, in this room, at this place where I am seated.

Recollection: I ask myself: Where do I stand in my family life / religious community, in my profession / ministry, in my dealings with others? What is the image of God that accompanies me? How do I feel in the community of believers? What are the ideals that guide me, the feelings which surface in me, my motivations and expectations? What causes pain and remorse in me? What are the inner blocks? I look at myself, as I have become over the years.

Inner image: I let myself go on the spiritual journey towards the inner divine space. I surrender myself unconditionally to the divine presence in me. I allow the divine Spirit to transform my being from within.

I.2. Sit Earthed

After having taken note of the *place* where I am now, I can trustfully enter upon the inner spiritual pilgrimage. It is important that one remains deeply united with the entire reality during the inner journey. Spiritual transformation does not take one away from the social and cosmic context of life but relates one to the process of life at a deeper level.

Reality is concretely represented to us through the earth. The earth is not just inert matter that we humans can indiscreetly utilize or boundlessly exploit. The earth is the life-bearing mother base of our existence. According to the biblical creation myth, God created the first man from the earth (*adamah*) and hence man is called Adam, which means 'formed out of the earth'. A piece of earth waking to consciousness – that is the human being. Our body is formed out of the earth; it is constantly being nourished through the earth and it will finally return to the earth. If our body is earth, the earth is the extended form of our body. The earth is our mother, source of nourishment and matrix of life. We are offsprings of the earth. All the food that we eat – cereals, vegetables, fruits and pulses – are gifts of the earth; these are in fact transformed earth. The water that we drink comes from the veins of the mother earth. Trees are like the hands of the earth stretched out towards us with food. Even our thoughts and feelings are registered in the energy field of the earth.

The earth is also the *body* of God. Through the earth the life-giving power and presence of the divine Spirit nourishes us. The earth binds us humans with one another and with the Divine as well. The earth is God's gift to us and our responsibility too. Since the earth is our life-base, we are duty bound to protect it for the future generations. Since the earth is our common home, the goods of the earth are to be shared with all. When our earth is exploited through the greed of a few, and millions are deprived of food and water, the dignity of mother earth is violated. And when the earth is constantly being poisoned due to the production drive of industries and avarice of merchants the future of the earth – and of humanity – is in peril. Respect for the earth, concern for the environment and genuine gratitude for life as well as a simple life-style characterise an earth-bound spirituality. Authentic spirituality makes us conscious of our responsibility towards the earth.

The earth is our mother,
We are her children

Atharva Veda 12.1.61

God entrusted the earth to human hands
to cultivate and care for it.

Gen. 2: 15

Meditation

Posture: I sit straight and relaxed, preferably on the floor, close to the earth. I become aware of how my body presses on the cushion / seat, how my legs touch the mat / floor.

Recollection: All my attention is brought downward. Slowly I feel into the earth. As a baby sitting on the lap of mother I sit on the ground and sense the life-bearing energies of the mother earth. I become aware of the oneness between my body and the earth. I sit gratefully and joyfully with the realisation that my body is transformed earth. I also feel myself closely united with all that grows out of the earth: humans, animals and birds, plants and trees. I sit in harmony with lakes and rivers, hills and plains.

Inner word: Interiorly I repeat: *my body is earth, earth is our body.* I try to resonate with the silence of the earth.

I.3. Sit Rooted

Be present to the present moment - such is the call of meditation. For this it is important to sit rooted in the earth; sit like a tree: straight, still, firm, relaxed and alert. The archetypal symbol of the tree is a help to enter into deep silence. What grows makes no noise - this is the silent message of a tree. Trees are like the hands of the mother earth folded in silent prayer towards the heavens.

The tree is a primordial symbol of human life. On the tree the twofold direction of human existence can be discerned: rootedness and relatedness. Out of rootedness in the Divine we grow in relatedness to all beings. The entire cosmos is like a tree, of which the Divine is the unseen, mysterious root of being. "Out of him we come forth, through him we grow, to him we return" (Tait. Up. 3.1). Through meditation we get more rooted in the Divine and intensely related to all beings. And this happens in the silence that the tree embodies.

If we go to a tree and ask, what the time now is, the tree would answer: it is *now*! The tree lives always in the present. "From the present to the present a tree grows." (Saint-Exupery). To be fully present, to be totally here and now – this is the meaning of meditation. The mind pulls us either to the past or pushes us to the future; the mind can hardly be present to the present moment. But the introspective faculty (*buddhi*) points to the depth of the present. Through the mind we elevate nature to culture; through the buddhi we explore the divine depth of this creative process. In meditation one tries to enter into this inner realm of perception. It is like getting in touch with the root of our being. Hence it is a help to sit like a tree while meditating: silent and alert, rooted and related.

All Holy Scriptures use the symbol of the tree to describe the holistic spiritual unfolding of the humans. At the beginning of the Bible stands the Tree of Knowledge (Gen. 2:9) and at the end of the Bible there is the Tree of Life (Rev. 22:14). The just man of Israel is compared to a tree planted on the banks of a river (Ps. 1). In the Upanishads a human being is compared to a tree (Brih. Up. 3.9.28) and the sage of wisdom is portrayed like a tree (Tait. Up. 1. 10). Jesus describes life in the Divine with the symbol of a tree (Jn. 15:5). In Buddhism the tree is the symbol of the enlightened one. Quran speaks of the heavenly tree the oil of which makes the divine lamp burn (24:35). The symbol of the tree deepens our consciousness in meditation as we move from the extrovert mind to the introspective buddhi.

Be still, my soul,
these trees are praying
                Rabindranath Tagore

If you know,
how to listen to trees,
you attain wisdom
                Hermann Hesse

Meditation

Posture: I sit straight and relaxed, preferably on the floor, close to the earth. Slowly I bring attention downward. I sit grounded in the earth.

Breathing: With every out-breath I feel how roots grow from my body into the earth; with every in-breath I feel how the life energy of the earth flows upward into the pelvic cavity. Further I feel the energy rising along the spinal cord like the vital sap of a tree flowing upward along the stem.

Inner image: Throughout the meditation I sit like a tree with the inner image: *I am like a tree rooted in the earth and related to all beings.*

I.4. Be in the Body

Sitting like a tree in resonance with the stillness of the earth brings in a deep silence. Meditative silence is not just abstaining from speech or overcoming distractions but an intense experience of bodily silence. One experiences the power of silence permeating the whole body. It is not a matter of the body that one has, but the body that one *is*. The body is the totality of being and behaviour through which one unfolds oneself. The body is the mode of being present to others. In and through the body one enters into relation with persons and things and thus realises one's true self. The body is what *I am* in the world.

The body is the primordial language of humans. Through the body I realise who I am, and share with others what I am. In my body I discover my own history with its lights and shadows. As I accept my body, I accept myself. A conscious and loving acceptance of my body means an integral self-acceptance. The basic cause of much of the physical illness and emotional conflicts is that we do not really respect our body and take care of it. When the body is instrumentalised through hyper activity and sense gratification or misused as a consumer object it revolts through all sorts of sickness. And when the signals of the body are ignored, one tends to develop chronic diseases, alcoholism, promiscuity and perverse addictions. Developing a positive and sacred relationship with the body could be an antidote to much of the disorder in our life.

There are three major spheres in the body: the mental, the emotional and the vital. Anatomically, these are associated respectively with the head, the heart and the abdomen. When one sits straight and relaxed, all the three spheres of the body come to a vertical harmony. A conscious and loving awareness of these three spheres deepens the bodily silence in meditation. One could start with the vital sphere: one enters the abdomen consciously and remains there respectfully feeling through the various organs in it.

It may be an experience of entering the prenatal phase and the infancy period or even getting in touch with the primal motherliness in one's being. It could mean a painful or joyful experience: old reminiscences and suppressed feeling may come to the fore. Several experiences of the first three years of childhood, of which one is hardly aware of, may surface. What one's mother and father meant in this formative phase of life may come to awareness. It is important to let these feelings flow freely; do not suppress them. Ultimately this is a liberative experience. Getting in touch with the vital centre of the body gives a biological basis to spiritual process.

> *Our body is earth*
> *waking to consciousness.*
> Chand. Up. 3.12.3.

> *God formed man*
> *from the earth*
> *and breathed into his nostrils*
> *the breath of life*
> Genesis 2:7

Meditation

Posture: I sit straight and relaxed, preferably on the floor, close to the earth. I sit grounded in the earth.

Inner image: After getting rooted in the earth, I bring the awareness to the earth that I am, ie. my body. I first become aware of the vital sphere of my body. Consciously I enter into the abdomen and feel through all the abdominal organs. I stay with each part with love and respect. I accept my body as it is now.

Recollection: I stay within the vital sphere anchored at the navel centre and become aware of the emotional reactions and inner movements. I take special note of the feelings associated with the prenatal / infancy phases of my life and those related to the early contacts with my parents. I let these feelings flow freely; this may mean a release of inner tensions and a joyful acceptance of my being-in-body.

Inner word: Interiorly I say to myself constantly: *My body is sacred.*

I.5. Feel through the Body

The body is a sacred reality. The body is the primordial place of experiencing the Divine. Before we go to rituals, symbols and scriptures in search of God we should first experience the touch of the Divine in our body. At the root of Christian faith there is the experience: " The Word became flesh" (Jn. 1:14; I. Jn. 1:1)). If God came to us through the body, we should first go to God through the body. If God met us in the body, we should meet God in the body. The body is "the temple of God" (I. Cor. 6:19). The body is the primal sacrament: the first place of God-man encounter. The body is the "abode of the Divine" (Bh. Gita, 13:2). Our body is God's *body*, for the supreme Spirit enlivens and moves it from within (*antaryāmin*, Brih. Up. 3.7.16-23). Hence our body is a matter of primal concern (*śarīramādyam khalu dharmasādhanam*).

Jesus experienced the liberative presence of the Divine in his body and he wanted to communicate this experience to all. "When your body is filled with light, with no trace of darkness in it, it will be light entirely, as when a lamp shines on you with its rays" (Lk.11:36). Jesus experienced himself as the Light of the world, and he reminded us that we too have to realise that we are the light of the world. This realisation is not just a matter of mental perception but much more a transparency experience in the body. The body has to be sensed as a translucent prism of the divine Light, as a transparent medium for the transforming presence of the divine Spirit. The Buddha experienced in his body the intense breakthrough of the Light from within and hence he could become an enlightening way to others.

In the process of meditation one could experience one's body as the sacred space of divine presence. This would lead to a bodily self-acceptance: I accept my body as it is with all the vitalising energies and the sickly elements as well; I accept my biography as it is engraved on my body. With this bodily self-acceptance much of the tension may get released and several inner blocks may be removed. This can in the long run mean a healing experience. An in*carn*ational spirituality has to have a bodily base, a biological reference.

When I accept my body with love, I deal with others respectfully. I can then accept others in their bodily dimension: in the concrete way in which they are. A bodily self-acceptance emanates positive vibrations which lead to healing in inter-personal relationships. Beyond that I am enabled to look at the material nature as a sacred space. The earth is the body of the Divine, and all that grows from the mother earth form a single family, in which one nourishes the other. I am thus motivated to deal with the things of nature with love and gratitude, with respect and responsibility.

> *Know that your body is*
> *the temple of God.*
> *Glorify God*
> *in your body.*
>
> I. Cor. 6:19-20

> *This body is the temple of God,*
> *in which divine consciousness abides*
>
> Bh.Gita 13: 2

Meditation

Posture: I sit straight and relaxed, firmly grounded in the earth.

Inner image: I feel through the entire body. I move slowly from the vital sphere downward through both the legs towards the feet. Gradually I return to the vital centre and then move upward towards the shoulders and further down into both the hands. It is important to start every movement from the vital centre, so that one gets stabilised at the centre.

Recollection: It is an exercise of becoming aware of the different parts of the body and finally of the organic unity of the body. One feels through the body with great respect and devotion, joy and gratitude. If my body is the *temple of the divine Spirit*, I make an inner pilgrimage through this sacred space that I am. I feel intensely the healing power and transforming presence of the Spirit in my body.

Inner word: Throughout the meditation I let the word resound in me: *my body is the temple of the Spirit*. (I Cor. 6:19-20)

2. The Breath

The bodily silence can be deepened through an attentive breathing exercise. As one becomes aware of the breathing process, consciousness sinks in a twofold way:

1. From the awareness of the body to the awareness of the spiritual realm. Breath energy (*prānah*) is the cosmic life-force that enlivens the body, and the energy-stream that transforms consciousness as well. Pranah is conveyed through air, the gross material element (*vāyu*), and at the same time it is the subtle life-energy. Hence through breath one experiences the transition of consciousness from the material to the spiritual, from body to soul. The pranah energy that streams forth up and down along the spinal cord activates the energy centres (*chakras*) on the spinal chord.

2. From the active I-centredness to the receptive Self-awareness. When one brings awareness to the breathing, one realises: I do not breathe, *it* breathes. Then one does not cling on to the *I* as the subject of all activities, but lets consciousness sink to the awareness of the divine Spirit as the true subject of being: the breath of God breathes in me. This gives rise to inner freedom in the process of meditation.

In these meditations one does not practice the yogic *prānāyāma*, where the breathing process is systematically controlled, but one just becomes aware of the breathing process. It is rather a receptive exercise of observing the breath.

The Exercises:

1. I breathe in gratefully and breathe out with confidence.
2. With every out-breath I feel the flow of the pranah energy permeating the entire body.
3. With every breath I feel the stream of pranah moving upward and downward along the spinal cord
4. With every out-breath I feel how the pranah energy flows from the spinal cord into the feet and the hands and the head.
5. I sit like a fountain and experience how the pranah energy streams forth beyond my body towards the world outside.

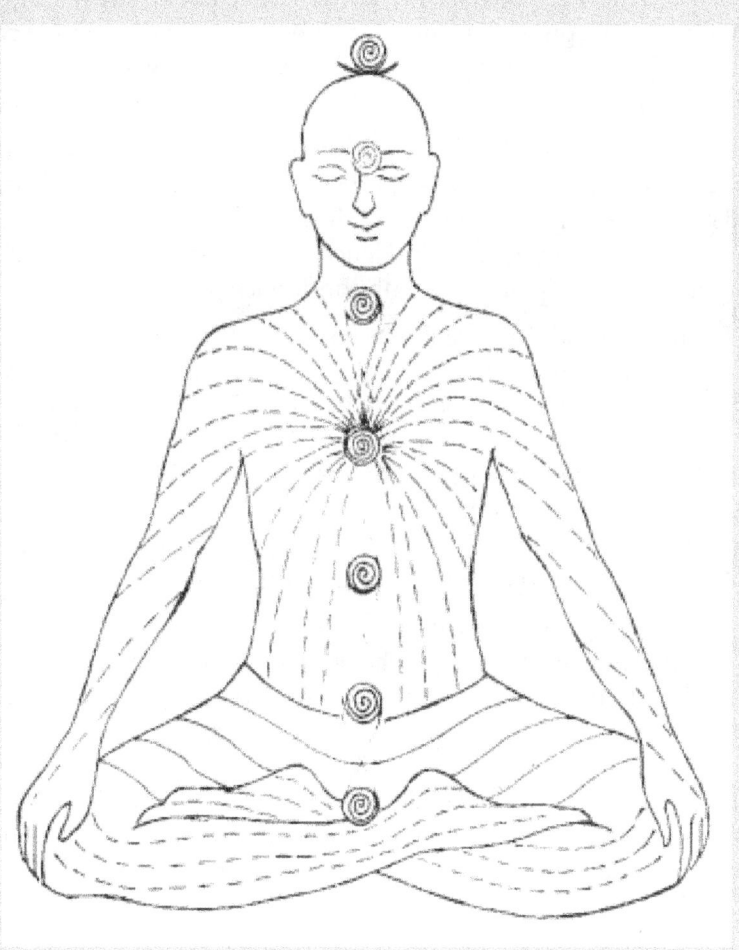

II.1. Feel the Breath

As the body comes to stillness through awareness, one becomes conscious of the movement caused by breathing. The energy that is absorbed through breathing is pranah. It is the life-energy that percolates through all beings in different degrees of intensity. All living beings breathe, even the earth and the ocean breathe. Pranah flows into us and streams through us. We breathe through all beings. Our life evolves in the cosmic stream of pranah. As fish in water we 'live and move and have our being' in the ocean of pranah.

Breathing in and out is the basic rhythm of life. Every time we breathe out, we die: out-breath is a pre-experience of the final exhalation, which could happen at any moment. Every time we breathe in, we are reborn: in-breath is the cosmic gift of life. Hence we should be able to breathe in with gratitude and breathe out with confidence.

Breathing is the mirror of the psyche: as we breathe, so we are. When we are disturbed through intense fear or anger, we gasp for breath. When, on the other hand, there is serenity in us we breathe smoothly. With emotional perturbance breathing becomes rather shallow and jerky; in moments of inner peace breathing goes deeper and harmonious. This being the case, one could through conscious and relaxed breathing get interiorly composed and serene. Hence the recommendation in meditation to spend some time becoming aware of breathing.

When I bring awareness on breathing, I realise that I am not the one who breathes in and out. I am not the real subject of breathing. It is not in my freedom to breathe or not. *It breathes*. I can only gratefully become aware of this life-process: how the pranah energy flows into me and streams through me. This makes me feel a deep inner freedom. I realise that I am not really bound up with my assertive I; there are deeper realms of consciousness. Here I find myself in a process of transition from the small I to the true self, from possessive mind to receptive buddhi, from the greed of having to the joy of being, from willing to happening, from speaking to listening, from doing to letting-go. Thus I create space within my consciousness for the divine Breath (Spirit) to transform my life; rather I feel myself led to the inner divine space where the Spirit constantly recreates my life. Meditation means alertness to the Spirit in me, *here and now*.

*The mind and all the senses are
woven on the breath.*

Chand. Up. 2.11.1

*Man is a creature of
borrowed breath*

Wisdom, 15:16

Meditation

Posture: I sit straight and relaxed, rooted in the earth.

Breathing: After becoming aware of the body, I bring my awareness to breathing. I breathe in and out in a relaxed mood without in any way trying to change the rhythm of breathing. Occasionally I may take a deep in-breath and a long out-breath. I breathe in with gratitude: let the gift of life freely flow in. I breathe out with confidence: let go. Gradually I come to inner serenity in which I feel intensely united with all beings around me. I breathe through them. I am in them, they are in me.

Recollection: If it is a help I mentally count while breathing: breathing in with 1.2., and breathing out with 1.2.3.4. I stay with the inner feeling: *I do not breathe, it breathes.*

II.2. Feel the Stream of Breath

It breathes! What is this *it*? Who breathes in us? This inquisitive question was raised by the wise men of Israel and by the sages of India. In both the spiritual hemispheres the answer they received was the same: God breathes! In the cosmos, in and through us, it is the divine Breath that streams forth. The word that is used in most classical languages for the divine Spirit literally means breath: *ruah* (Hebrew), *pneuma* (Greek), *spiritus* (Latin), *ātma* (Sanskrit), *āvi* (Tamil) and *chi* (Chinese).

In the second creation myth of the Bible we read: "God formed the first man from the earth and breathed into his nostrils the breath of life" (Gen. 2:7). The out-breath of the Creator became the in-breath of the creature. After breathing into Adam God did not withdraw but his breath continues to breathe into creation, just like the hidden springs of the mountain continuously giving birth to a river. The entire cosmos lives and evolves out of the breath of the Divine (Is. 42:5). "If God were to take back his breath from our nostrils, we will all return to dust" (Job, 34:14-15). "If you stop their breath, they die and revert to dust. If you give out your breath, fresh life begins. You keep renewing the world" (Ps. 104: 29-30). "It is God who gives breath and life to all beings" (Acts, 17:25). We humans survive on a 'borrowed breath' (Wis. 15:16). These sayings do not divinise the material breath but uphold that through pranah we experience the gift of life that ultimately comes from a divine source.

Jesus addressed God as Father. The Aramaic invocation *abbo* literally means: the well-spring of the primal life-breath. Jesus was not referring to a patriarchal figure enthroned above the clouds, but experiencing the Divine as the primordial fountain of life within him. (Jn, 5:26).

In Indian spiritual heritage *prānah* is experienced as the divine life-energy (*prāno Brahmāh*, Chand. Up. 4.10.4). Everything is enlivened by the constant flow of divine pranah (*antaryāmin*, Brih. Up. 3.7.16). We humans experience the Divine as 'breathing in and through us´ (Kena Up. 1. 9). The Vedic sage prayed: "Oh, Pranah, you shall not be hidden from me, nor be estranged from me. I bind you onto me for sustained life. I hold you in my body like the enlivening fire" (Ath. Veda, 11.4.26). The stream of pranah is divine nectar (Brih. Up. 2.5.4), divine face (Tait. Up. Santimantram), divine body (Chand. Up. 3.14.2), the primal source of nourishment (Chand. Up. 5.2.1), and the beginning and end of the universe (Tait. Up. 3.3).

Everything has its origin
and sustenance
in the breath of God
>Atharva Veda 11.4.1

It was God's breath
that made me,
and keeps me alive
>Job, 33:4

Meditation

Posture: I sit straight and relaxed, rooted in the earth.

Breathing: After feeling through the body, I bring my awareness to breathing. I breathe in and out relaxed without in any way trying to change the rhythm of breathing. Occasionally I may take a deep in-breath and long out-breath. While breathing in, I gratefully let the gift of life flow into me. While breathing out, I feel the pranah energy streaming into the whole body: first toward the feet, then into the hands. Gradually I feel all the cells of my body *watered* by the stream of pranah.

Recollection: With this conscious and relaxed breathing I feel my body as a sacred space enlivened by the continuous breath of the Spirit.

Inner word: In every breath I remain recollected with the word: *the breath of God breathes through me* (Job, 27:3).

II.3. Feel the Energy Centres

The pranah energy supplied through breathing reaches every cell of the body through the *nādis*, the subtle channels of energy distribution. The Indian masters speak of 72.000 nadis percolating the human body. The main nadi is the *suhumna*, with its two side tracks, *ida* and *pingala*, all running though the spinal cord. Along the spinal cord the pranah energy constantly flows upward and downward *watering* the entire body with the pranic energy. In this spiral movement the seven energy centres (*chakras*) open up along the spinal cord.

The Chakra	The Location	The Reality	The Colour	The Energy
7 Sahasrāra	Cerebral plexus / cranium	Unmanifest	Violet	transcending
6 Ajna	Pineal plexus / brain-centre	Manifest	Indigo	realising
5 Viśuddha	Carotid plexus / throat	Space	Blue	communicating
4 Anāhata	Cardiac plexus / heart	Air	Green	unfolding
3 Manipura	Solar plexus / navel	Fire	Yellow	forming
2 Swādhisthāna	Hypogastric plexus / genitals	Water	Orange	purifying
1 Mūlādhāra	Pelvic plexus / spine-base	Earth	Red	stabilising

One shall not force open any chakra through powerful breathing or mantra, but shall allow the pranah energy to flow smoothly along the spinal cord. In this receptive process one or the other centre may open up emanating the respective energy vibration or colour. Ultimately it is a matter of divine grace. It is important that the three lower chakras be stabilised before one goes upward. It may be a help to stay longer at the heart chakra (*anāhata*) and feel the energy vibrations of divine love emanating from there. Later one could focus attention on the brain chakra (*ajna*) and feel the divine light emanating from there.

The spinal cord is the axis of the microcosm that the human person is. It connects the heavens with the earth. The ethereal energies are united with the telluric powers in a creative process of fertilisation. Through meditation one is thus integrated to the entire cosmic process of birthing. A new consciousness is born in the bodily silence of meditation.

> *Your body will be*
> > *full of light,*
> > > *as a lamp brightens up*
> > > > *your inner recess*
> > > > > Lk. 11:36

> *Realise the*
> > *Divine within your body*
> > > *as pure, effulgent Light*
> > > > Mund. Up. 3.1.5

Meditation

Posture: I sit straight and relaxed, preferably on the floor, deeply rooted in the earth.

Breath: After feeling through the body and after feeling the stream of the pranah energy in all parts of the body, I bring attention to the spinal cord. I try to feel the flow of the pranah energy along the spinal cord. With every in-breath I feel the upward flow and with every out-breath I feel the downward flow along the spinal cord. I observe how the different chakras are activated and eventually one or the other being unfolded. Whenever I feel that one or other chakra is hyper activated, I try to bring attention to the earth that would absorb the excess energy flow.

Inner word: In every breath I remain recollected with the word: *the breath of God breathes through me* (Ws. 15:16).

II.4. The Body in Becoming

Our body is not a static reality. It is rather a dynamic whole, a flowing reality. Every moment the body changes. The body that I am at the beginning of the meditation is not the body that I am at the end. In every breath the divine-cosmic energy flows fresh into the cells and these are renewed. With every in-breath we are re-born. The human body is like a fountain. From the spinal cord the revitalising pranah energy gushes into the entire body through the 72000 nadis. Our body is an ever becoming process.

It is good to realize this dynamic character of the body in meditation. It is a help to perceive its transient character and its translucent nature as well. Through the pranic dynamic process the divine Spirit transforms human body constantly into the *temple of the Spirit*. Pursuing this process would mean that the mind follows the energy flow of the pranah. The mind is controlled by the pranah. (Chand. Up. 4.3.3). The breath is the absorbing and revitalising matrix of all senses. As the mind serenely follows the pranah stream in the body, one attains a dense and alert bodily silence.

In this silence consciousness sinks from mind to buddhi, from extrovert perception to introspective intuition, from a fragmentary analysis of reality to a holistic vision of the mystery of life. *I do not breathe, it breathes*! Gradually the fixation of the *I* as subject of activity at the mental level gets reduced. Consciousness is sensitivised for a deeper insight into true subjectivity at the buddhi level.

When I become aware of the stream of the pranah energy in the body as the percolation of the divine energy, my body gets charged with divine life. When I realise that 'the breath of God breathes through me' I am on the way to a deeper mystical subject-consciousness: ultimately it is the divine Spirit that lives and acts through me. In as much as the passion to possess and control everything gets reduced, one creates inner space for the divine Spirit to transform the human spirit.

Breath is the door of the heart,
on the way to the Divine.

Chand. Up. 3.13.1

The breath of God
breathes through me

Job, 27:3

Meditation

Posture: I sit straight and relaxed, preferably on the floor, rooted in the earth.

Breathing: After getting rooted in the earth I feel through the entire body. Gradually I bring awareness to the spinal cord and feel the upward and downward flow of pranah along the spinal chord.

Breath: With every in-breath I feel the upward flow and with every out-breath I feel the downward flow of the pranah energy along the spinal cord.

Inner image: When the pranah energy gradually flows serenely along the spinal cord, I feel myself as a fountain. With every in-breath I feel the pranah energy flowing upward along the spinal cord, and with every out-breath I feel the energy flowing from the heart chakra downward into the legs and the hands. I sit like a fountain. It could be a help to feel how the pranah energy is transformed into the energy of love or joy or light. The whole body is thus experienced as watered by the love or joy or light of the divine Spirit.

Inner word: In every breath I remain recollected with the word: *the divine life / love / joy / light streams through me.*

II.5. In Harmony with All

The breath is the life-dynamic of the universe. In the process of breathing all are bound together. Breathing binds us with every living being, and also with every thing in nature. The earth and the mountains breathe, the ocean and the rivers breathe, rocks and stones breathe. Everything is dynamised at the subatomic level by the power of pranah. In the one universal stream of pranah all human beings are interrelated, and we are connected to the rest of creation. We are in a cosmic web of pranah. Individuals are brought into harmony with the totality of the cosmos. Through breathing we realise that we are parts of an evolving universe. No human person, no living being, no material reality, nothing is independent of others. Everything nourishes everything else. Everything breathes through everything else. Everything is branch of everything else on the cosmic tree. The divine breath breathes through all like the vital sap of this tree. Awareness of breath leads to a deep mystical sense of cosmic inter-dependence and to an ethical sense of global responsibility. Meditation deepens this sensitivity.

In human persons the evolution of consciousness has reached a higher stage. The spiritual power dormant in matter unfolds to a higher state of consciousness in us humans. The human life is bound up with the material realm, but human consciousness gets elevated above the material and is made open to the Infinite. Human creativity is rooted in the fertile ground of *nature*, but the human soul unfolds diverse forms of *culture*. Man is anchored in the earth, but open to the heavens. This twofold orientation of human life can be perceived in breathing. The energies of the earth rising from below are fertilised by the powers of the heavens coming from above. This fecundation takes place in the human body, specifically along the spinal cord. In meditation we realise that our existence is stretched between these two poles. This means the integration of the feminine and masculine energies, the union of the *yin* and *yang* principles, the harmonising of *ida* and *pingala* along the spinal cord: the wedding of *śakti* and *siva* in the subtle body. This integrating process takes place in all beings. But in the human this is elevated to a conscious participation in the cosmic process of life. By feeling the stream of pranah in the body and beyond the body one gets intensely attuned to this cosmic process of life.

Pranah is the Lord
of the universe.
He permeates everything
and keeps all in being.

Atharva Veda, 11.4.1

It is God who gives
life and breath to all;
in him we live and move,
and have our being.

Acts, 17:25-28

Meditation

Posture: I sit straight and relaxed, preferably on the floor, rooted in the earth.

Breathing: I feel through the entire body. Slowly I bring awareness to the spinal cord and feel the upward and downward flow of pranah along the spinal cord. With every in-breath I let the pranah energy flow upward along the spinal cord, and with every out-breath I let the energy flow from the heart chakra downward into the legs and the hands. Gradually I feel how the energy vibrations flow beyond my body to the world outside.

Inner image: I sit like a water fountain. I feel my spinal cord like the upward flow of the fountain, and my entire body being *watered* by the pranah energy. Further I feel how this cosmic energy that gushes into me, streams through me out into the world around. My body becomes a transparent medium of percolation for the cosmic life-energy stream. I find myself within the cosmic process of the divine energy stream.

Inner word: Throughout the meditation I remain recollected with the word: *from my vital centre emanate streams of living water* (Jn. 7:38)

3. The Word

With the awareness of the body and breathing, the mind slowly comes to a certain stillness. But the inner psychic elements with all the shadows and negativities may cause road-blocks on the inner journey. One gets stuck in the past or worried about the future. One becomes aware of the negative forces like greed, envy, anger and vengeance, the tendency to depression etc. One feels as if wandering through a *dark night*. In order to overcome these inner disturbances the classical spiritual masters recommend that one evokes healing vibrations in the psyche: (i) through the repetition of a key word, (ii) through the practice of praying the name of the divine Lord, and (iii) through the repetition of a mantra.

With this an inner switch-over takes place: from mind to buddhi, from the objectifying way of thought to the introspective way of awareness. Gradually one is brought to the threshold of the *heart*. "Go into your inner space and commune with the Divine therein", Jesus said (Mat. 6:6). All names and forms, images and symbols of the Divine step back. "There the eye does not reach, not speech, nor mind" (Kena Up. 1.3). One is gradually led by the divine Spirit into the sacred space within. Here one becomes aware of the Divine as pure presence: be present to the present moment! One cannot force this entry through exercises; one can only keep oneself open for this: "The Divine reveals itself to the one whom it chooses" (Katha Up. 1.2.23).

The Exercises:
1. With every out-breath I take a key word, which helps a deepening of the inner silence.
2. In loving surrender I repeat the name of Jesus with every breath
3. In inner alertness I repeat the mantra OM with every out-breath
4. With deep compassion I feel how the vibrations of OM spread beyond my body into the surroundings and bring me in harmony with all.
5. I linger serenely in the inner silence and remain present to the present moment.

III.1. The Key Word

A basic problem we have to bear with in the meditation exercise is distractions. Even after meditating for long years one may have to put up with these disturbing elements. All sorts of thoughts and feelings storm into us and take us away from the path of concentration. There are two types of such distractions:

1. Issues of our current life situation may intrude constantly in meditation on certain days. These need attention. It is good to spend a few minutes at the beginning of meditation to attend on them with serenity and compassion. One can then take note of the message these have for oneself.

2. There are the stray thoughts and passing feelings which break in at any moment in every meditation. These are in fact unimportant matters which distract attention on the inner path. Fighting with such nuisances is not helpful. One should rather learn to live with them. As the Zen master says, one can imagine that these distractions are like clouds drifting past a mountain peak, occasionally letting a few drops fall; however the mountain remains undisturbed. What is important is that one sits serene with inner resoluteness and preserves the interior freedom.

In order to stay interiorly recollected it is recommended to take one word that could bind the thoughts and deepen the consciousness. The word shall have only one or two syllables, so that it can be rhythmically repeated with every out-breath.

Some such words are: *śānti, shalom, peace, mercy...*

Such a word having a dense spiritual content must evolve from within and give a clear impulse to the inner process. The purpose is not to reflect on the meaning of this word, but to resonate with it for deepening the inner stillness. One repeats the word with every breath with a certain inner rhythm. Constant repetition of a word is not what the mind likes to have; so the mind lets it fall. Consciousness sinks to deeper levels. The rhythmic repetition of the word with breathing creates positive vibrations within. One sits with the awareness that the pranah energy flows filling the body with the content of the word that one takes in, like, *peace, mercy...*

Go on repeating
    a key phrase (mahāvākya)
        with inner attentiveness
            Sivananda of Rishikesh, Sadhana, 97

Select a short word
    and take it deep into your self.
        Cloud of Unknowing, 4

Meditation

Posture: I sit straight and relaxed.

Breathing: I get rooted in the earth and feel through the body. With every in-breath I feel the pranah energy flowing upward along the spinal cord, and with every out-breath I feel the energy flow from the heart chakra downward into the legs and the hands, into the whole body. I sit like a fountain.

Inner word: With every out-breath I say interiorly the key word. The word is repeated with an inner rhythm prolonging it into the space of the out-breath.

Recollection: I feel the stream of breath as the energy of peace, joy, mercy…percolating the body. Thus the bodily silence is deepened and filled with a spiritual content. The distractions gradually vanish. Slowly I am led to the inner sacred space where I experience the Divine as the subject of my being.

III.2. The Divine Name

The transition from mind to buddhi inevitably takes the sadhaka through the psychic realm, where all sorts of repressed feelings and unfulfilled desires are registered. These appear in symbolic forms in dreams, and come up as distractions during the meditation too. Confronted with them in the inner jungle of the subconscious one feels let down or lonely, excited or confused. This may also suggest an absence of God: God has forsaken me! This inner state may last for quite some time as the *dark night* of the soul.

What is important in such a crisis is to resort to deep confidence: trust in the divine master who never leaves us but accompanies us through this darkness. The only way out is to surrender ourselves totally to the divine master within us. This can be done through a simple but effective method: repeat the name of the divine master. The name is the means of invoking the presence of the other. One lets oneself be guided by the Divine. One inserts oneself unconditionally to the divine process.

Repeating the divine name is a universal form of prayer found in all religious traditions. Hindus chant e.g.: *Om namah Śivāya* or *Om namō Nārāyanāya*. Buddhist repeat: *Buddham śaranam gacchāmi* or *Om mani padma hum*. Muslims pray the 99 names of Allah. Often this is all done with the help of a *mālā* of sacred beads or a prayer wheel. A divine name is charged with divine energies and hence its repetition produces healing vibrations in the psychic realm. Several disturbing elements of the subconscious are removed and thus the inner path to the divine depth is cleared.

We Christians repeat the name of Jesus on the inner journey. Jesus is the *way* to the divine depth and the *light* on our way. Hence by repeating devoutly and trustfully the name of Jesus we surrender ourselves to the guidance of the divine master who lives deep within us. Jesus accompanies us on the inner journey not from outside but from within the depth of consciousness. Christ is the healing presence of the Divine within us, here and now. He leads us from loneliness to communion, from darkness to light, from fear to love from estrangement to oneness with the Divine (*hesychia*). The *Prayer of the name of Jesus* has been a monastic as well as popular form of prayer that started with the Desert Fathers (3-5 centuries) and evolved in the Eastern Churches through Sinai (5. cent), Athos (14 cent) and Russia.

The practice of this simple form of prayer can lead one to an abiding sense of being *in Christ* in daily life and work.

> *Remain in the devout repetition*
> *of the name of Jesus Christ,*
> *so that the heart absorbs the divine Lord*
> *and the Lord captures the heart:*
> *both become one.*
>
> John Chrisostom, PG. 60, 75

> *I am easily attainable to the one*
> *who bears me unceasingly in the heart*
> *with a single-minded devotion*
>
> Bh. Gita, 8:14

Meditation

Posture: I sit straight and relaxed rooted in the earth. I keep my left palm touching the heart-centre and the right hand laid open on the knee; or else both the hands laid open on the knees.

Recollection: Through the awareness of the body and of the breathing I come to a bodily silence. I look deep into myself and perceive my inner journey through the jungle of the psyche. I bring to awareness some of the shadows and blocks which come up on the inner path.

Inner word: Taking refuge in Christ the divine master, who lives in me, I repeat the name *Jesus* with every breath. With every out-breath I repeat the name *Jesus* prolonging it into the breath, or I say mentally *Je-* in in-breath and *sus* or *sum* in out-breath; or else, I say mentally *Christus* in in-breath and *Jesus* in out-breath. Some other forms which could be repeated with the out-breath are: *Om namō Christāya* (I venerate Christ), *Jesu Om... Jesu, Jesus Christ have mercy on me*. It is important that the name is repeated with a certain melody so that the psyche comes to resonance with the divine presence. With every in-breath I feel the divine energy of Christ streaming into me and with every out-breath this spiritual energy percolating the body and permeating my life-situation.

III.3. The Mantra OM

Mantra is something subtler than a word or a name of the Lord. Mantra is a sound that brings about inner harmony. Mantra is that by which the mental state is transcended (*mananāt trāyate iti mantra*) and deeper levels of perception are awakened. The repetition of a mantra creates integrative vibrations in the inner realms of the mind and psyche, and consciousness is brought to the intuitive level of the buddhi.

Of all the mantras the primal mantra is OM. It is the combination of three syllables: A, U and M (Mand. Up. 8). A is the first sound that we produce; hence every alphabet begins with A. M the last sound that resounds as humming when the mouth is closed. U is the middle sound. Hence AUM – spoken as OM – refers to the totality of reality: the beginning, middle and end of all. OM is therefore the sound symbol of the Divine that permeates and comprehends all, transforms all into One. (Praśna Up. 5. 5). "Pranah percolates with the sound OM" (Chand. Up. 1.5.3).

Through the meditative repetition of OM one gets attuned to the divine vibrations in the deeper realms of consciousness. With the inherent three sounds a transition of awareness happens: from A through U to M, from mind (*manah*) through psyche (*chitta*) to buddhi, from wakeful state (*jagrit*) through dream state (*swapna*) to intuitive awareness (*sushupti*) (Mand. Up. 9-11). The Divine is experienced beyond the personal objectification in names and forms, and intuited as the transpersonal subject: as the Ground of being, as the ultimate Self (Brahman), as the transforming Spirit (Atman). Invoking the name of the divine master in the previous meditation led to an intense I-thou relationship and devotion. Repeating OM here leads to a deep mystical union. "OM is Brahman" (Maitri Up. 6.3; Katha Up. 2.16).

In the Christian experience, this would mean that one enters through Christ the inner master into the inner-trinitarian dynamics of divine life. "It is an OM which emerges from the Silence of the Father, opens up in its depths for the uttering of the Word, and concludes ineffably in the Spirit. It is an OM, which sings at once all the inner movements of God towards himself and also all this inner repose within himself" (Abhishiktananda, Saccidananda, 189-90). Through OM one attunes oneself to the groaning of the Spirit within.

Sink into the divine Self
with the mantra OM.

Mand. Up. 2. 2-6

The Spirit groans from our hearts
in a way that cannot be expressed in words.

Rom. 8:26

Meditation

Posture: I sit straight and relaxed, deeply rooted in the earth.

Breathing: In the bodily silence I feel with every in-breath the upward flow of the pranah energy along the spinal cord, and with every out-breath the downward flow into the body.

Inner word: With the flow of the pranah energy from the spinal cord into the body, I repeat OM. With the in-breath I feel the energy of the divine sound streaming into me and with every out-breath I feel the percolation of the OM vibrations in the entire body. It is important to repeat the mantra aloud with every out-breath; slowly the voice gets lower and lower ending in an inner humming. This finally merges into a vibrant silence.

Recollection: I stay in the dense stillness that comes through the meditative repetition of OM. As much as possible I let no thoughts and images enter this silence. I sense the divine Spirit that groans wordlessly from within my heart. I feel myself inserted into the inner-trinitarian process of life and love.

III.4. The Cosmic Tone

The divine presence that is intuited through OM permeates the entire realm of creation. Hence the mantra OM not only brings about an integrative process within, but also leads to an intense experience of harmony with the cosmos. The deeper one gets attuned to the divine vibration within, the more one comes into harmony with the creative melody of the universe.

"In the beginning was the Word (*Logos*), and the Word was divine; everything has been created through the Word" – The Gospel according to John begins with this cosmic vision. "In the beginning was the Sound (*śabda*), and the Sound was divine; everything has been created through the Sound" – thus the Upanishadic sages describe their cosmic vision (Chand. Up. 1.1.2; 1.5.1-5). The divine silence is articulated through the sound OM resounding in the cosmos (Maitri Up. 6.22). "Everything is OM" (Chand. Up. 2.23.3). Everything is vibration – this is the insight of the sages; and the primordial vibration is OM.

Modern physics confirms this insight of the ancient sages: reality is vibration; matter is energy; the entire universe is a flux. We live and move in the cosmic stream of energy. The subatomic realm of the electronic field is an immense movement. The dynamics of this movement is the divine vibration, which is perceived as OM.

With the meditative repetition of OM one gradually feels that the OM vibrations flow beyond one's body and self. One gets tuned to the cosmic melody. A deep oneness with all things in the universal divine stream of life and love is felt. The meditation with OM opens the buddhi to a cosmic consciousness. It is a sort of expansion of consciousness beyond oneself. Meditation then becomes sensing the divine pulsation at the heart of the universe. With it one overcomes loneliness and estrangement; one can resonate with the entire reality. A deep compassion towards all beings is the consequent grace.

"The contemplation of Saccidananda comes to rest in the secret utterance of OM, the sacred syllable which stands for the whole mystery of Being, the movement from fullness to fullness, the repose of fullness in fullness:

> *OM, Fullness here, fullness there; from fullness proceeds fullness; take fullness from fullness, fullness ever remains!*"

(Abhishiktananda, Saccidananda, p. 189)

The entire cosmos is
set in movement through OM.
Chand. Up. 1.5.1

Everything has been created
through the Logos
Jn. 1:3

Meditation

Posture: I sit straight and relaxed, deeply rooted in the earth

Breathing: In the bodily silence I feel with every in-breath the upward flow of the pranah energy along the spinal cord, and with every out-breath the downward flow into the body. Further I feel how the energy vibrations flow beyond my body to the world outside.

Inner word: With the flow of the pranah energy from the spinal cord into the body, I repeat OM. With the in-breath I feel the energy of the divine sound streaming into me from the universe, and with every out-breath I feel how the OM vibration permeates my body and the world around me as well. I repeat OM aloud to sense its resonance; gradually the voice gets reduced and the repetition ends in a vibrant silence.

Recollection: I sit in deep communion with all beings outside. I feel how from my heart-centre vibrations of love emanate and flow into beings outside. The divine Spirit of love emerging from the indwelling Trinity flows through me into the world like a fountain. I experience a divine harmony with the universe.

III.5. The Eternal Now

As the repetition of OM ends in a vibrant stillness one enters the divine depth of silence. Here everything disappears: words and symbols, names and forms, melodies and mantras. All personalised images give way to a transpersonal experience of the transcendental unity of reality. Vedantic sages demand that one should go beyond all names and forms through a negation process (*nēti nēti*). Christian mystics too uphold the *via negativa* that would say *no* to every image of God (*nada nada*). Zen masters call for a total emptying of the mind (*mu*). Jesus himself invites us to 'go into the inner room' and to 'close the door' to all external images and names so that we can 'commune with the Father in absolute silence' (Mt. 6:6).

There is only deep silence where one is alone with the One, the human self alone with the divine Self, the soul alone within the Spirit. Even the sense of duality between these two vanishes. The individuality of the human self is not annihilated, but transformed into a mystical consciousness of utter oneness with the One, total transparency to the Divine. Mystics of the East and of the West compare this state to the merging of rivers in the ocean (Mund. Up. 3.2.8; Teresa of Avila, Interior Castle).

Brahmavid Brahmaiva bhavati – the one who knows the Divine becomes divine (Mund. Up. 3.2.9). *Quisque Deum intelligit, Deus fit* – the one who knows God becomes God. (Thomas Aquinas). Only in oneness with the Divine do we really experience the Divine within and around us. This is a fundamental insight of all mystics. *Aham Brahmāsmi* – I am Divine, says the Hindu Vedantin (Sankara). I am being divinised, says the Christian mystic (Origen). I am the God, whom I love, says the Muslim sufi. (Al-Hallaj). This experience of the *divinisation of the human* (*theosis*) seems to be the most intimate experience of mystics and hence the deepest meeting point of religions.

Realize that we are *divine*, realise that the divine Spirit is transforming our life into divine life – this is the call of meditation. This realisation is a matter of divine grace for which the human can prepare through ascetical life and disciplined meditation. It is an experience of inner enlightenment: the light within shines forth. In this divine light one looks deep into the present moment. Eternity is the divine depth-dimension of the *now*. Be fully present to the present moment – this is the way to the perception of the eternal now (*nunc aeternum*).

Father, you have hidden these things
  from the learned and the clever,
    and revealed them to mere children
                                                Mt. 11:25

To whomever Brahman is not known,
to him it is known.
  To whomever it is known,
    he does not know it.
      Brahman is not grasped by those who claim to grasp it;
        it is understood rather by those who do not understand it.
                                                Kena Up. 2.3

Meditation

Posture: I sit straight and relaxed, deeply rooted in the earth

Breathing: In the bodily silence I feel with every breath the upward and downward flow of the pranah energy along the spinal cord, and then in the entire body.

Inner word: With the repetition of OM together with the key word (eg. OM santi) or the name of the Lord (Jesu OM…Jesu) I come to a deep silence. Slowly I notice how the word / name / OM merges into an empty but vibrant silence.

Recollection: I become gratefully conscious of the inner sacred space in me, empty of all images and thoughts: no name, no symbol, no mantra. Time stands still. There is only a sense of being present to the present moment, being in a totally receptive mood awaiting the divine light, being open to the movements of grace within, being transparent to the divinising energies of the Spirit. All that matters is alertness to the divine depth of the *now*. Here I let the divine Spirit take over.

PART II
Symbols of Silence

4. The Fountain

Meditation is the way to the divine centre of our being (*meditari*). It is a receptive process: we do not force a specific state of consciousness in us, but we become increasingly conscious of the integrative process that is happening deep within. The healing presence of the divine Spirit in us is like an inner fountain that opens up at the divine centre of our being. Through the meditative inner journey we open ourselves to this fountain; we let the divine well open; we get the blocks cleared so that the divine stream transforms our entire being.

The Church Fathers and Christian mystics describe the dynamics of the Trinitarian process in us with the symbol of a fountain. The Father, like a hidden *well-spring*, unfolds through the Son, the *divine well*, and pours out the Spirit, the *divine stream*. In meditation one comes to the realisation that 'from the centre of the body streams of living waters pour forth'. (Jn. 7:38).

Jesus spoke expressly of the vital centre of the body (*koilia*). Hence we should feel in a bodily way the life-giving power and presence of the Spirit. The words of the **Gospel of John** and the imageries of the Church Fathers could accompany us on this inner journey. Meditating on the mystical symbols of this Gospel will take us to an inner process that makes us realise that we are called to participate in the divine self-consciousness of Jesus.

The Exercises:

1. With great confidence I enter upon this inner journey
2. In deep silence I experience the Father as the hidden divine spring in me.
3. With gratitude I put my trust in the indwelling Christ, who opens the divine spring
4. In union with all beings I feel the Spirit as the life-giving divine stream
5. With joy I experience how the divine stream flows through me.

The numbers in brackets refer to the Gospel of John.

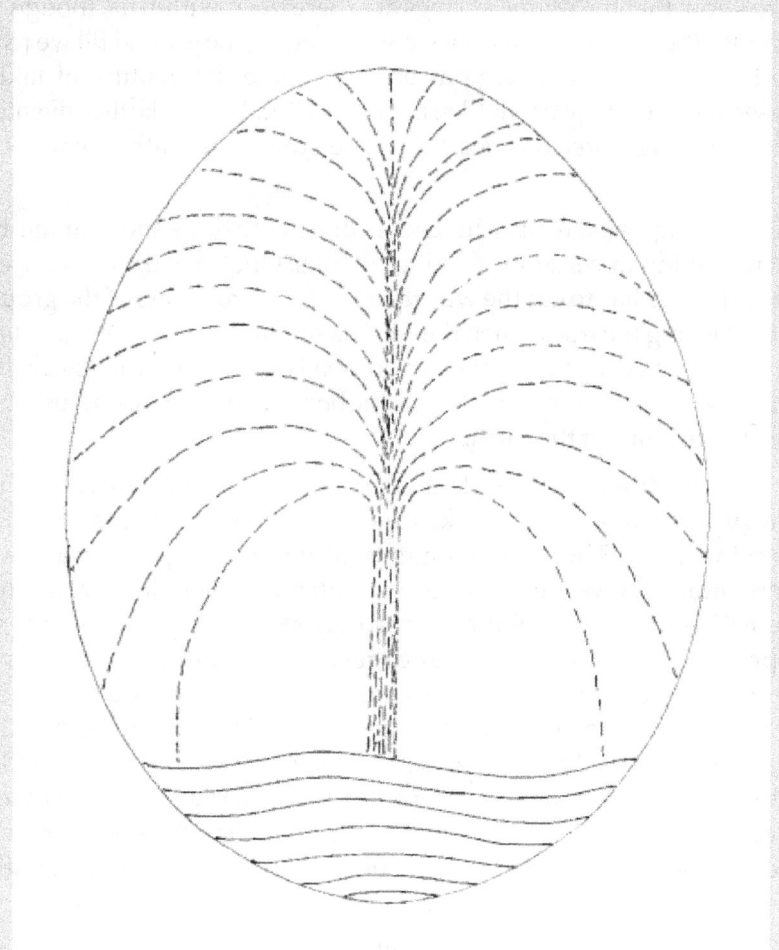

IV.1. The Way to the Depth

The spiritual life is a process of discovering and realising the true self that is hidden within the divine space in us. It is like entering a deep cave inside, utterly dark, yet full of light; it is like digging a well to reach the hidden spring, that eludes human grasp, yet ever present. Faith enables us to know that the divine springs are there deep within us, though we don't see them. With great trust we start digging the ground till we reach the hidden water source. Spiritual life is like the venture of taking possession of the treasure hidden in the field (Mt. 13:44), like the adventure of discovering a precious pearl concealed under the path. (Chand. Up. 8.3.2).

Digging a well is an arduous task done with hope and courage, but often meeting uncertainties and hardships. One feels the resistance of the earth; one has to cut the way through the hard layers of the ground but not losing the track when the earth is soft and watery. One must not stop the search with an inner cistern nor shall one give up while struggling with rocky layers. With resolute will one burrows deeper till one discovers the hidden veins of the earth.

The meditative journey to the experience of the inner divine spring is a process like this. It takes us through the diverse levels of consciousness. There are moments of joy and hope, courage and consolation. But we must also reckon with moments of inner resistance. We will be confronted with the hard layers of our psyche where we experience blocks though undigested ill-feelings, unforgiven reminiscences, unfulfilled desires, long-lasting wounds, acute aggressivity, oppressive guilt feelings, life-eroding addictions and other negative powers. There is no point in suppressing them, nor is it a help to analyse them one after the other in detail. We will never succeed in disposing of them all. While digging a well one does not stop with every stone analysing its contents; one has to continue digging with a basic acceptance of the soil with its specific characteristics.

Psychology is definitely a great help to analyse the sub-conscious dynamics and locate the inner blocks in the spiritual process. But psychology cannot offer integral healing. The healing energies emanate from a deeper level of consciousness: that of the divine Spirit welling up like a hidden spring in us. Healing comes when we dig the inner well deep unto the divine well-spring, when we open our heart to this divine fountain, when we let the streams of the Spirit flow through us.

He who holds on to his life,
loses it.
He, who lets it go, will keep it
unto eternal life.

Jn. 12:25

Meditation

Posture: I sit straight and relaxed; I feel the rootedness in the earth.

Breathing: In the bodily silence I feel with every breath the upward and downward flow of the pranah energy along the spinal cord, and further in the entire body. (see. Ex. II. 4)

Inner image: I imagine my inner spiritual journey like digging a well in my consciousness. With great trust in the Spirit in me I sit with a *let go* feeling. I take note of the positive movements in my psyche: hope and joy, courage and enthusiasm. I also become aware of the negative forces blocking my inner way: feelings of revenge and envy, woundedness and aggressivity, greed and anger. I just become aware of all these as ingredients of the terrain of my psyche without judging them or evoking unnecessary guilt feelings. I accept myself as I have become over the years. I accept myself as accepted by God. I let myself be guided by the divine Master in the process of digging the *well* in the terrain that I am, digging for the hidden divine springs in me.

Inner word: Interiorly I tell myself constantly: *the one who walks with me shall not walk in darkness* (Jn. 8:12)

IV.2. The Father as the Hidden Spring

The inner experience that Jesus had is the light in which a Christian sadhaka makes the inner spiritual journey. Jesus experienced himself as the well that opens the hidden springs of the Divine. In speaking to the Samaritan woman at Jacob´s well, Jesus pointed to himself as the divine well (4, 14). On the feast of the Tabernacles too Jesus presented himself as the fountain of divine waters (7:37). The well is an archetypal symbol that takes us to Jesus´s intimate relation with the Father. With this symbol we could interpret the mystical meaning of several key expressions of Jesus about the Father:

> I draw life from the Father (6:57)
>
> The Father who is the source of life, has given the Son to be the source of life (5:26)
>
> I come out of the Father (16:28).
>
> I am sent forth by the Father (10:36; 7:28; 17:3)
>
> The one who sent me is in me. (8:16, 29)
>
> I am in the Father, the Father is in me. (14:10, 20; 17:21)
>
> The Father and I are ONE. (10:30; 17:22)

These sayings point to the experience that the Father is the hidden spring of the Divine. Just as the well experiences the hidden springs Jesus experienced the Divine within him. "The Father is the fountain of the Son´s being" (Ambrose, PL, 16, 642). With the term *Father*, Jesus is not pointing to a patriarchal God enthroned far above the world, but the motherly-father, the generating matrix and nourishing base of his divine nature. The Son 'clings on to the feeding breast of the (motherly) Father' (1:18). The Father is the divine source of Jesus' Son-consciousness. The Father is the *that-out-of-which* of the Son. The Father is the incomprehensible mystery dimension within the Divine. "No one has ever seen the Father; no one has ever heard his voice" (5:37). The Father is the true *subject* of the Son: "The words which I speak are not my words; the Father speaks through me" (14:10, 24; 12:49-50). Jesus experienced the Father as a well experiences the hidden springs. This could be our experience too. Jesus wanted to make us partakers of his inner experience:

> Just as I draw life from the Father, you will live through me (6: 57)

Just as I am sent forth by the Father, I send you (17:18).

Just as I am in the Father, and the Father is in me, I am in you, and you are in me (17:21; 14:20).

Just as I and the Father are one, may you all be one in us (17:21-22).

Through the inner process of digging the well into the deeper realms of consciousness we come gradually to the experience of the Divine as the well-springs deep within us. This is the way one could experience the Father. Jesus initiates us to this: Go into the silent depth of your consciousness and therein meet the Father! (Mt. 6:6).

> *God has brought forth the Word*
> *as the hidden springs bring forth the river.*
>
> Tertullian, Adv. Prax. 4

Meditation

Posture: I sit straight and relaxed, rooted in the earth.

Breathing: With every breath I feel the stream of the pranah energy percolating in the body especially at the vital centre and in the pelvic cavity. The breath of God breathes through me. (see Ex. II. 2)

Inner image: In the bodily silence I become aware of my vital centre. There I visualise a living spring opening up. It pours out the stream of divine life. With every in-breath I feel how this spring is vitalised and with every out-breath I feel how this stream of divine life unfolds like a living fountain nourishing the whole body, the entire being. I experience the divine Father as the hidden divine spring in me.

Inner word: I focus attention of the word of Jesus: *I come forth from the Father* (Jn. 16:28)

IV.3. The Son as the Well

The well is a powerful archetype. This symbol is found in the Scriptures of world religions to describe the self-understanding of the saviour figures. Jesus uses this archetypal symbol to describe himself. (4:14; 7, 37). This symbol points to the deep relation between the Father and the Son in the Trinity.

The Son is the self-unfolding of the Father, as the well is the self-outpouring of the hidden springs. "The Son is born of the fountainhead of the Father" (Origen, On John 2.2.10). The Son is the self-manifestation of the Father, the self-giving of the Father, the self-expression of the Father. The Son is the *ekstasis* of the Father, the Logos in fuller sense. The Son opens the divine life-source. The Son is the true image (*eikon*, Phil. 2:6) of the mystery that the Father is.

Through this self-outpouring of the divine springs creation evolves. Everything has been created in and through the divine Logos. In the Logos is the Life of the universe, for through him all things came to be. Through the Logos came forth the Light of human consciousness for the Logos enlightens the minds of all people in all cultures and religions (1:1-5). The Logos as the divine self-outpouring has been made manifest in a concrete and embodied way in Jesus Christ. In this sense Jesus is the manifestation of the divine *ekstasis*, the embodied form of the divine *kenosis*: In him the divine Logos became flesh (1:14). He is the Son of God. The well (or river) is the *son* of the hidden springs of the earth. As Son Christ is essentially one with the divine nature, yet distinct from the Father; one with the Father, yet one with us humans. Jesus is the face of God turned towards humanity, the self-outpouring of the divine well-springs. Hence the faith proclamation of the first disciples: you are the Son of the living God. (Mt. 16:16).

It is with the consciousness of being the Son, the well of the divine springs, that Jesus invites us 'to drink from him'. He is the *way* to the inner springs, the fountain of divine *life* and the *truth* that unfolds the hidden presence of the Divine. (14:6). When we trustfully let ourselves be led to this well, we realise that the divine well opens up in us. "Out of your vital centre shall flow streams of divine waters" (7:39). We are called to share in his consciousness of being the well: we are also called to be *wells* of divine life. "The water that I shall give will turn into a spring in you streaming out divine life" (4:14). He lives in us as the divine well that pours out the love of the Spirit into our hearts (Rom. 5, 6). Meditation is the process of reaching into this inner well, the process of realizing that we are wells of the Divine.

> *The Son goes out of the Father*
> *as the river flows out of the hidden springs.*
>
> Hippolitus, PG. 10, 817

Meditation

Posture: I sit straight and relaxed rooted in the earth. I come to a deep bodily silence.

Breathing: With every in-breath I feel the stream of the pranah energy flowing upward, and with every out-breath flowing downward along the spinal cord. (see Ex. II. 4)

Inner image: I experience the divine Father as the hidden spring in me. Gradually a well opens up unfolding the hidden spring. It turns out to be a living stream of love permeating my being. In it I experience the presence of Christ enlivening my body and soul. I let my inner blocks be removed and the negative energies be transformed by this stream of divine grace communicated through Christ. With every in-breath I feel how the well is nourished by the spring, and with every out-breath I feel how the stream of Christic consciousness deepens and integrates my inner awareness.

Inner word: With every out-breath I repeat the name of Jesus (see Ex. III. 2). Or else, I remain focussed on the word of Jesus: *come and drink from me* (Jn. 7:37).

IV.4. The Spirit as the Flow

The hidden springs open up as a well because of the current inherent in them. From still waters no well or river will come forth. The power of the current makes the hidden springs generate a well or a river. The power in the Divine is the Spirit. The divine Spirit immanent in the hidden springs of the Father makes the Father generate the Son as the well. The Spirit is the dynamism (*dynamis*, Acts, 10:38) that activates the divine well-springs. The Spirit makes the Son come forth as a well from the divine spring, the Father.

The Spirit 'reaches the depths of the Divine' (I. Cor. 2:10) and enables the self-unfolding of the Divine in the Son. The Spirit is the energy that makes the divine ground into a generating mother-base. The Spirit is the power of the divine fertility, the feminine dimension of the Divine: the birthing, caring and nourishing factor, the *motherliness* in the Divine. The Spirit is the wisdom that makes the divine silence articulate itself in the Word. The Father gives birth to the Son in the Spirit; the Father pours himself out through the Son in the Spirit. As the hidden spring, the well and the power of the current in a fountain, the Father, the Son and the Spirit are in and through one another (*perichoresis*): distinct, but not separate.

The Divine is triune - this means that the Divine is a self-giving reality. The Divine pours itself out continuously and we experience this as divine Love. Jesus does not point to a static, self-contained God above us, but to a dynamic self-outpouring God within us. And this self-outpouring of the Divine was what Jesus experienced intensely within himself. He felt that the divine spring of the Father opened in him and poured out the divine Spirit through him. His words and actions, his suffering, death and resurrection meant a salvific self-outflow of the divine stream into humanity.

Hence he could invite us to 'come and drink from him' (7:37). He wanted us to realise that the flow of the divine Spirit makes 'streams of living water spring forth from within our vital centre'. (7:38). He promised that 'the water that we drink through him would turn into a stream of divine life' (4:14). He expects us to participate in his mystical experience of constantly being born of the divine source. In this sense, he wanted us 'to be reborn in the Spirit that is divine water'. (3:5)

Give space to this transforming Spirit – this is the basic purpose of meditation. The Spirit takes us to deeper levels of consciousness, even to the 'depths of the Divine' (I Cor. 2:10-12). The Spirit is the one 'who prays from within us' (Rom. 8:26), the one 'who makes us free' (Gal. 5:16) and creative (I Cor. 2:11). The Spirit is the inner Teacher (I Cor. 2:13).

God has poured out his love
into our hearts
through the Holy Spirit.

Rom. 5:5

Meditation

Posture: I sit straight and relaxed, rooted in the earth. I enter into a bodily silence.

Breathing: With every in-breath I feel the pranah energy flowing upward along the spinal cord, and with every out-breath I feel the energy flow from the heart chakra downward into the legs and the hands, into the whole body. I sit like a fountain. (see Ex. II. 4)

Inner image: The divine Father is like the hidden spring in me. Gradually a well opens up unfolding the hidden spring. It turns out to be a living fountain of love (the Son) permeating my entire being. In it I feel the life-giving presence of the divine Spirit rising in me like a powerful fountain energising the whole being. With every in-breath I feel how the fountain is nourished by the divine spring; in every out-breath I feel how the stream of the divine Spirit percolates in me. The divine spring unfolds in me as the stream of the Spirit. The divine breath breathes in me as the breath of life.

Inner word: With every in-breath I feel the divine waters streaming into me from the Father through the Son in the Spirit, and with every out-breath I repeat OM (see Ex. III, 3) . Or else, I remain recollected on the word: *From your vital centre shall flow streams of living water.* (Jn. 7:38)

IV.5. We are the Channels

As we experience the divine spring (the Father) opening up as the well (the Son) and pouring out divine Love (the Spirit), we feel ourselves as the channels of the divine stream of love. Our being emerges from within the inner-trinitarian process. Our consciousness is enlightened by the Light of the Spirit. Our life evolves as a fountain streaming forth divine Life all around. The Divine is not just an object before us, but the ultimate subject within us. Thus we become channels of divine Life in the universe. In and through us humans the divine Spirit works in the world. Our thoughts and feelings will then be transparent to the transforming work of the Spirit. Our words and activities will transmit divine love. Our love will then be the sacrament of divine compassion. Through our presence we make the Divine present in the world. Here we realise: "When we are led by the Spirit, we are heirs of God, coheirs of Christ" (Rom. 8:14, 17).

As the bearer of the divine fountain Jesus said: "From your vital centre shall pour forth streams of divine life" (Joh. 7:39). The term is *koilia* (=womb), not *kardia* (heart).This indicates that the one who drinks from the divine well-springs will get impregnated by the divine Spirit. Fecund by the Spirit one shall give birth to the Spirit in the world. We are born of the Spirit, and we give birth to the Spirit. We are children of God and *mothers* of the Divine as well. (Origen, Gregory of Nyssa). "I give birth to the one who gives birth to me" (Eckhart). We become channels of the energies of the divine Spirit in the world. We become transparent prisms of the divine light, echoes of the divine Word, channels of the divine grace, branches of the divine tree, flames of the divine fire, waves of the divine ocean…

"The one who is united with Christ is one Spirit with him" (I Cor. 6:17). Our being is constantly being divinised; our life is being transformed into the divine life. This process is called the divinisation of the human (*theosis*) in classical Christian traditions: not that we humans *become* God, but that the human soul is being divinised. Know who you are: "called to be filled with the fullness of God" (Eph. 3:19); become what you are: "partakers of the divine nature" (II Peter 1:4) – this is the divine impulse of Christian faith. Meditation is a way to this spiritual self-realisation: Realise that you are divine!

But this means a great responsibility. If we are channels of the divine Spirit, our life has to be a constantly alert to the movements of the Spirit in us and around us. Our works of compassion, our solidarity with the poor, our commitment to the demands of justice, our concern for the protection of nature – all that would mean that we work with the Spirit in the making of the new creation. Thus we become effective instruments in the emergence of the Kingdom of God proclaimed by Jesus.

> *Out of the innermost divine springs*
> *I emerge as a fountain*
> *in the Holy Spirit*
>
> Meister Eckhart, M. 134.

Meditation

Posture: I sit straight and relaxed, rooted in the earth. I enter into a deep bodily silence.

Breathing: With every in-breath I feel the pranah energy flowing upward along the spinal cord, and with every out-breath I feel the energy flow from the heart chakra downward into the legs and the hands, into the whole body. I further feel the flow of the pranah energy beyond my body into the world. (see Ex. II. 5)

Inner image: I feel that a divine fountain opens up at my vital centre. With every in-breath I feel how this spring is vitalised and with every out-breath I feel how this stream of divine life unfolds like a living fountain nourishing the whole body, the entire being. The Spirit flows beyond my body making me a channel of divine love. I feel how my soul becomes increasingly transparent to the divine presence. My consciousness wakes to the realisation: *I am divine.*

Inner word: With every in-breath I feel the divine waters streaming into me from the Father through the Son in the Spirit, and with every out-breath I repeat OM (see Ex. III, 3) and thus get tuned to the divine life in me. I remain recollected on the word: *In me a divine fountain opens welling up to eternal life* (Jn. 4:14).

5. The Tree

A deeper rootedness in the divine ground of being and an intense relatedness to others, including the things of nature characterise the integral growth in spirituality. For this a tree is an archetypal symbol. The tree is a primordial teacher of humans. In this series of meditations we shall explore how the symbol of the tree interprets the mystery of the Divine as Trinity.

It is important that in meditation one identifies oneself with the tree. One discovers the archetype of the tree within oneself and *becomes* the tree. One has to experience the various aspects of the being and becoming of the tree within oneself. It is good to draw trees after inspiring meditations: one recalls the inner image of the tree as it came up clearly and draws it intuitively. This is done in a receptive mood: I do not draw the tree, but *it draws*. After drawing trees for a few weeks, arrange them in chronological order and spend some time observing the inner dynamics: what do these images of my inner world tell me?

It is good to take one tree in the vicinity as the spiritual master. Go to that tree at regular intervals, watch the tree carefully, listen to the tree, speak to the tree and pay attention to the silent message of the tree. It is also helpful to have a bodily contact with the master tree: lean on it, embrace it, climb on it, enjoy its fruits and shade. Thus one becomes part of the tree.

The images of the **Gospel of John and the texts of Church Fathers** will guide us in meditating on the symbol of the tree.

The Exercises:

1. I feel myself rooted in the ground of the divine Father
2. I feel myself being supported by the stem that the divine Son is
3. I feel the Spirit as the divine sap that flows through me
4. I feel myself as a branch that is being transformed through the divine stream of life
5. I feel how I am intimately bound with the entire universe as branches of a tree.

V.1. The Father as the Hidden Root

We humans love trees. The Tree is our primordial home. Sitting under a tree means getting back to the place where we came from. There are indications that the human body is a further evolute of the tree. Classical Indian (Katha Up.6.1-4) and Greek (Plato) thinkers describe the human body as an inverted tree (*arbor inversa*). From the root mass of the brain branch off the nervous system, the lymphatic system and the skeletal system. From the bronchial stem the bronchioles grow like tiny roots into the lungs. The cardiac system is like a root structure. A cross section of the kidney reminds us of a big seed. Placenta is quite similar to a plant. Since we bear a tree structure in our body, we feel at home under a tree. Our body, mind and soul get refreshed after a walk through the woods, because the trees emanate healing vibrations. There is a spontaneous fascination in us for trees. We love gardens and avenues, woods and forests. Trees make us feel that we are loved by the universe.

Jesus loved trees. He meditated with the silence of the trees on hilltops (Lk. 6:12). He taught under trees (Jn. 1:48). He told several parables with the metaphor of plants and trees (Mt. 13:4, 25; Lk. 13:6, 19; 21:29). If he were to write an autobiography, he may use the metaphor of the growth process of a plant (Jn. 12:24). And to describe his intimate relationship with humans, Jesus takes up the image of the vinestock and the branches (Jn. 15:5).

Jesus experienced the Divine as Father deep within himself as the stem experiences its roots. "I come forth from the Father" (Jn. 16:28). "I live through the Father" (Jn. 6:57). "The Father who is the source of life has made the Son the bearer of life" (Jn. 5:26). The mystical depth of such expressions could be better grasped if we read them in the language of a tree. The stem would speak of its roots: I am in the roots, the roots are in me; we are one. In his deepest divine consciousness Jesus said "I am in the Father, the Father is in me. The Father and I are one" (Jn. 10:30, 38; 14:10).

Jesus lived with a divine sense of being sent by the Father. The depth of this sense of mission could be understood in terms of the tree: the seed sends forth the sprout; the root sends forth the stem. "The Father sends forth the Son" (Jn. 5:36- 38). Jesus experienced the incarnate self-giving of the Divine. "The one who sent me is within me" (Jn. 8:16, 29). The root and the stem are substantially one, but distinct. The root does not become the stem, or vice versa. Father and Son are of one nature (*homoousios*), yet they are distinct.

The root is an archetype of the eternal mother. In his deep divine consciousness, Jesus experienced the Divine as the generating mother-base, as the *whence* of his being, as the inner root and well-spring, as the Motherly-Father. "The Son is begotten from the womb (*de utero*) of the Father" (Ambrose, ML. 16, 642).

> *The Father is the root of*
> *the Son's being.*
>
> Ambrose, PL.16, 642

Meditation

Posture: I sit straight and relaxed, preferably on the floor, close to the earth. I sit like a tree rooted in the earth. I come to a bodily silence.

Breathing: With every out-breath I feel how roots are growing from my body into the earth; with every in-breath I feel how the nourishing energies of the earth flow upward into my body. (see Ex. I. 3)

Inner image: I sit like a tree and feel how the stem senses its relationship with the hidden roots. With this I try to feel how Jesus experienced the Father as the root of his being.

Inner word: I remain recollected with Jesus's word: *I come forth from the Father.* (Jn. 16:28)

V.2. The Son as the Stem

The tree is a primordial source of blessing. The tree gives food and breath, shade and shelter, clothing and home. The tree refreshes our body and elevates our spirit. The tree heals physical ailments and provides psychic integration. Trees connect the earth with the heavens. Trees are born as the male energies of the skies fertilise the female powers of the earth. Trees are the offspring of the father-sun and mother-earth.

A tree brings blessings from above and makes the divine presence felt in our midst. A tree is the natural place of meeting the Divine. Primal people experience the power of the Spirit in trees. The sages of the Himalayas and the masters of China meditated and taught under trees. The Buddha received enlightenment under the tree. The Egyptian goddess spoke to the King through the sycamore tree. In the Semitic religions tree is often the medium of divine revelation. God appeared to Abraham under the oak of Mamre (Gen. 18:1). Yahweh revealed himself to Moses through the burning bush (Ex. 3:2). The angel of God called Gideon under the terebinth tree at Ophrah (Judges, 6, 11). David heard the voice of the Lord in the tops of the balsam trees (II. Sam. 5:24). The Hebrew name for God, *Elohim*, and the Arabic name, *Allah*, are derived from the root *el/al*, which refers to *elon*, meaning the tree. Tree is a primal language of divine revelation.

Jesus understood himself as the stem that unfolds the mystery of the divine roots. "I am the vine stock" (Jn. 15:5) "I come out of the Father" (Jn. 16:28). "I draw life from the Father" (Jn. 6:57). "The Father has sent me forth" (Jn. 8:42). The root points to the hidden mystery of the Divine (Jn. 5:37); the stem refers to the revelation of the mystery (Jn. 14:7). The stem is the *son* of the root, the self-unfolding of the root. The Son is the self-giving of the Father, the self-revelation of the Father. Jesus lived in this divine consciousness of being the Son of the Father. Hence he could say: "The one who hears me, hears the Father" (Jn. 14:10); "the one who sees me, sees the Father" (Jn. 14, 9). "the one who knows me, knows the Father (Jn. 14:7). "I am the way to the Father" (Jn. 14:6). "I perform the works of he Father" (Jn. 5:36). In his deepest divine consciousness Jesus said "I am in the Father, the Father is in me. The Father and I are one" (Jn. 10:30, 38). The mystical depth of the divine self-understanding of Jesus can be better grasped if we hear these words as coming from the stem that he represents.

> *God has brought forth the Word*
> *as the root brings forth the shoot.*
>
> Tertullian, Adv. Prax. 4

Meditation

Posture: I sit straight and relaxed, preferably on the floor, close to the earth. I sit like a tree rooted in the earth. I come to a bodily silence.

Breathing: I bring attention to the flow of the pranah energy along the spinal cord. With every in-breath I become aware of the pranah flowing upward and with every out-breath I feel the pranah energy streaming forth from the heart centre downwards into the entire body. (see Ex. II. 5)

Inner image: I sit like a tree and feel how the stem senses itself as emerging from the hidden roots. The spinal cord is felt as the stem with the immanent flow of life energy. From the root of the divine Father the Son emerges as the stem. I feel Christ as the stem / vine stock in me. I identify myself with a branch and feel how I am supported and enlivened by the stem that Christ-in-me is.

Inner word: With every breath I repeat the name of Jesus (see Ex. III. 2), interiorly dwelling on the words: *abide in me; I abide in you* (Jn. 15:4).

V.3. The Spirit as the Vital Sap

From time immemorial one finds in all cultures the symbol of the invisible cosmic tree. The entire universe revolves around it. It is the axis of the world (*axis mundi*): it gives the universe strength and stability, fecundity and integration. The cosmic tree takes its root from the abysmal well-springs of the earth and grows towards the sky bringing down the blessings of the heavens. There is a constant fusion of the fertilising power of the earth and the enlightening energies of the sun on the cosmic tree. It was termed Osiris in Egypt, Vorukasha in Persia, Aswatha in India, Kien-mu in China and Yggdrasil in the Germanic tribes.

Every tree is a miniature form of the axial cosmic tree. A tree grows out of water sources and preserves the water element in nature to sustain life. It transforms water to sap and juice and thus prepares food for living beings. Trees are like the extended hands of the mother earth offering food and drink. The invisible life-giving energies of the universe percolate through trees and nourish all living organisms. Trees embody the motherly element in nature. By transmitting the sap of life trees are living symbols of the power and presence of the divine Spirit.

Jesus experienced the outflow of the divine stream of life through him. If the Father is like the root and the Son like the stem, the Spirit is like the vital sap that flows from the root through the stem. Just as the vital energies pour themselves out from the hidden depth of the root through the stem, the Spirit emerges from the Father and streams forth through the Son. Jesus experienced himself as the channel of the divine Spirit. Hence the call: "He who is thirsty, let him come and drink from me. From his vital centre shall flow streams of living water. With this Jesus meant the Spirit" (Jn. 7:3-39). Life reaches its fulfilment only `when one is reborn in Spirit and water´ (Jn. 3:5). Water is a primordial symbol of the Spirit.

The Father generates the Son in the Spirit. The Spirit is that which enables the Son to be born of the Father. The Spirit is the immanent power of the Divine (*dynamis tou theou*): the power of life and love, the power of oneness between the Father and the Son and the power of distinction as well. The Spirit is the self-giving of divine love (Rom. 5:5), the self-communication of divine life (Jn. 6:63), the self-outpouring of divine springs (Jn. 7:38), the self-manifestation of divine light (Acts 2:3), the self-revelation of divine truth (Jn. 14:17).

The Spirit proceeds
like the sap proceeding
from the root
through the stem

Tertullian; Adv. Praxean 8

Meditation

Posture: I sit like a tree, straight and relaxed, rooted in the earth.

Breathing: With every in-breath I bring attention to the upward flow of the pranah energy along the spinal cord and with every out-breath to the downward flow. Further I feel how the pranah energy flows from the heart centre to the entire body. The breath of God breathes through me. (see Ex. II. 5)

Inner image: I sit like a tree and sense how the stem and the root feel the percolation of the vital sap in them.

Inner word: With every in-breath I feel the divine sap flowing into me from the Father through the Son in the Spirit, and with every out-breath I repeat the mantra OM (see Ex. III. 3). I remain recollected on the word: *We drink from the one Spirit* (I Cor. 12:13).

V.4. We are Branches in the Divine

The tree is a primordial teacher of humanity. The primal peoples still draw the wisdom of life from trees: they listen to the oracle of the higher spirits on sacred trees. They have their places worship in groves under sacred trees. Important decisions are taken under auspicious trees. "One learns more from trees than from books" (Bernard von Clairvaux). Tree deepens our consciousness and broadens our perspectives.

Jesus lived out of the consciousness of being the divine stem (Son) unfolding the divine root (Father) and communicating the divine sap (Spirit). The divine Spirit that emerges out of the Father and flowing through the Son streams into us. Hence Jesus said: "I am the vine stock and you are the branches" (Jn. 15:5). Humans are like branches growing out of the divine stem that the Son is.

What then is the difference between the relationship of the root with the stem and that of the stem with the branches? The same vital sap flows from the hidden depths of the root through the stem into the branches. The same divine Spirit that filled Jesus enlivens us too. The divine Spirit makes us partakers of the divine life. There is only one outflow of divine life: from the Father through Christ into us. Hence Jesus said:

> Just as the Father sent me, I send you into the world (Jn. 17:18).
>
> Just as I live through the Father, so you live through me (Jn. 6:57).
>
> Just as the Father loved me, I love you (Jn. 15:9; 17:26).
>
> Just as I abide in the Father, you will abide in me (Jn. 15:10).
>
> Just as you Father are in me, and I am in you, they must be in us (Jn. 17:21)
>
> Just as the Father and I are one, may you all be one: fully one (Jn. 17:23).

The repeatedly used preposition just as (*kathos*) points to our existence in grace: we live the divine life. If we are branches of the divine tree, our life evolves not outside the Divine, but within the divine dynamics of life. We live in Christ. Christ lives through us. Who am I? – with this question go to a tree; listen to the answer that the tree gives: you are a branch of the divine tree. This gives us a deep self-understanding and self-esteem. We realise that we are like drops of the divine ocean (Teresa of Avila), flames of the divine fire (John of the Cross), sparks of the divine fire (Meister Eckhart), parts of the divine body (I Cor. 12:12). We are daughters / sons of God (Rom. 8:14), heirs of God, coheirs of Christ (Rom. 8:17). Our life evolves in the divine process. Our being is constantly divinised (*theosis*). Meditation is a way to realise this divine transformation process happening deep within us. It is like a branch becoming aware of its inner dynamics on the tree.

> *The Spirit of Christ*
> *reinstates the divinity in us*
> Cyril of Alexandria, PG. 75, 1088

Meditation

Posture: I sit like a tree, straight and relaxed, rooted in the earth.

Breathing: With every in-breath I bring attention to the upward flow of the pranah energy along the spinal cord and with every out-breath to the downward flow. Further I feel how the pranah energy flows from the heart centre to the entire body. The breath of God breathes through me. (see Ex. II. 5)

Inner image: I sit like a tree and identify myself with a branch. I feel how the branch feels vertically the inner flow of the vital sap, the anchoring in the stem and the rootedness through the stem. With this I sense the indwelling Spirit streaming forth into me from the divine Father through the Son. I feel how the flow of he Spirit continuously inserts me to the life of the root (Father) through the stem (Son). I realise that my life evolves within the trinitarian life-process.

Inner word: I remain recollected on the word: *I am a branch of the divine tree* (Jn. 15:5).

V.5. We are Branches of One Another

Tree is a living symbol the harmony between unity and diversity. The entire tree is one, but there is a fascinating diversity on the tree: no two leaves are exactly the same. The one vital sap flows through the whole tree creating manifold forms and colours. Respect diversity and recognise unity – this is a basic message of the tree. This is the fundamental principle of social fabric in human life. The otherness of the other has to be accepted and respected; at the same time the deeper bond of unity has to be admitted and promoted. The other person can be genuinely respected only when one is aware of the deeper oneness. The mind looks at the other as *thou*, but the buddhi intuits the oneness between *I* and *thou*.

A tree is a living symbol of utter generosity. On the tree everything is shared with everything else. The nourishment that is prepared through photosynthesis by every leaf is shared with all other parts. No leaf lives for itself, it lives for others; no branch grows by itself, it grows through others. The entire tree lives not for itself, rather it gives itself away fully: flowers and fruits, sap and leaves, root and stem, shelter and shade. The tree reminds us that self-giving adds quality to human life. Life evolves in love. Human existence is co-existence.

A tree is a living symbol of social life and responsibility. If we all are branches of the one divine tree, we are branches of one another: each one nourishes the other, each one lives through the other. Harmony in social life demands a spiritual awareness of the divine love that deeply binds our hearts and totally transforms our life. On this Jesus said: "As the Father loved me, I have loved you" (Jn. 15:9). "As I have loved you, you should love one another" (Jn. 15:12). Love is a divine energy that emerges from the Father, flows through the Son and streams through us in the Spirit. What binds our hearts together is ultimately `the love of God that is being poured into our hearts through the divine Spirit´ (Rom. 5:5). God in us is the real subject of true love. "The love with which the Father loved me, should be in you" (Jn. 17:26). Here inter-personal relations get a divine depth and sacred meaning. In genuine love we experience through other persons how intensely we are loved by God. Through love we are led to the *sacred space* deep within the *I* and the *thou*. Such a mystical perception enables us to face conflicts and tensions in relationship.

Life in society means a sacred responsibility: the call to work for the integral welfare of all. Sharing one's life with others and committing oneself to social well-being, concern for justice and care for the environment are consequences of a spirituality of solidarity. With these we grow together as branches of one another; nourished by the one divine Spirit we bear flowers which brighten up our life, and fruits which bring about a new creation.

> *Love one another*
> *as I have loved you.*
> Joh. 15:12

Meditation

Posture: I sit straight and relaxed like a tree, interiorly united with all beings.

Breathing: I feel how the pranah energy flows along the spinal cord, and from the heart-centre into the body. Further I feel how the energy streams forth beyond my body. I breathe through other beings; they breathe through me. I feel the deep bonding in the one stream of this cosmic-divine energy of life. (see Ex. II. 5)

Inner image: I sit like a tree and identify myself with a branch. I feel how intensely the branches are bound together in the one stream of vital sap. With that I sense how deeply I am related to human persons and bound with all other beings in the one divine Spirit, in the one divine stream of love, in the one divine flow of life, in the one divine process of transformation.

Inner word: I recall interiorly certain persons / things and sense the deep bonding with them. I remain recollected on: *We are all branches of one another and for one another.*

6. The New Life

It was Paul who gave a theological foundation to faith in Christ. On the way to Damascus Paul went through a deep conversion experience, which meant for him a total transition from the old way of religiosity to a new vision-and-way of life. During his three year long *retreat* in the Arabian Desert he reflected on what this meant for him and for humanity at large. The transition from the old to the new has been the basic framework with which Paul reflects with zeal and consistency.

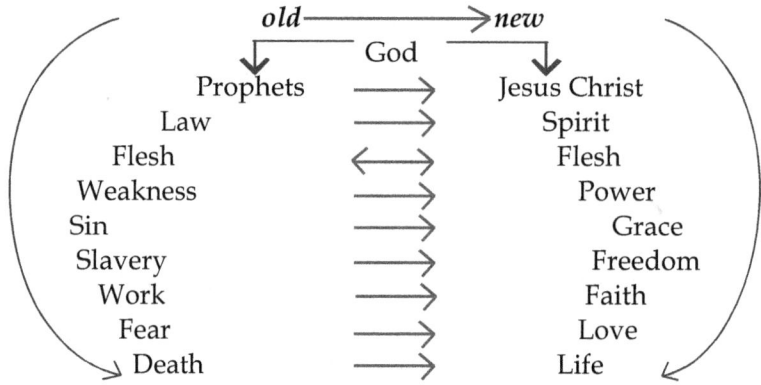

The polarity between these two streams is not just something of the past but it reveals what is happening in the present, in the *now* of our life; it is not just a perception confined to the experience of Paul, but it is a process that takes place in the life of each person. In this series of meditation we shall pursue this process with some key texts from **the Letters of Paul**.

The Exercises:

1. Life in flesh: where a life determined by the Law leads to
2. God in flesh: what God has done to lead us to salvation
3. Life in Christ: the graced state to which we are called
4. Life in the Spirit: the dynamics of divine transformation in us
5. Divine Life: signs and values of the life guided by the Spirit.

VI.1. Life in Flesh

1. *"God* wants everyone to be saved" (I. Tim. 2:4) – this is a basic premise of Paul's theological vision. For this God has instilled the natural light of reason and guidance of conscience in everyone (Rom. 1, 20). But often humans took to 'futile thoughts and filthy enjoyments' which distanced them from God (Rom. 1:21-27).

2. In order to lead humans to 'a full knowledge of the truth' (I Tim. 2:4) God gave the *Law* through the *prophets*. "The Law is holy and what it commands is sacred" (Rom. 7:12). But the Law reached the *flesh*, by which Paul means the existential fragility and *weakness* of humans. "Because of the frailty of the flesh the Law could not do what it was meant for" (Rom. 8:3).

3. Dwelling on his own past life, Paul says that the Law could only make us aware of our sinfulness (Rom. 3:20). "When Law came, *sin* got revived" (Rom. 7:9). "Sin took advantage of the commandment to evoke all kinds of evil inclinations in me" (Rom. 7:8).

4. A blind adherence to the Law only makes us bonded to empty religiosity and hence *'slaves* of sin' (Rom. 6:16). One is then forced to a compulsive observance of the Law by doing *works* to please the law-giver God. "No one can however be justified before God by doing works of the Law" (Rom. 3:20).

5. The Law could not liberate us humans from the bondage to sinfulness; hence we live in *fear* while fulfilling the demands of the Law. "It is the spirit of bondage that brings fear into our life" (Rom. 8:15).

6. And ultimately, Paul argues, the Law can only lead us to *death*: to alienation from the divine source and goal of life. "While we were in the flesh, our sinful passions, which were aroused by the Law, were at work in the members of our body, only to bear fruit to death" (Rom. 7:5). Law evokes sin; sin causes death (I. Cor. 15:56).

What Paul here portrays is not just the picture of a foregone phase of life before the coming of Christ; it is rather an honest probing into the dynamics of sinfulness presently operating in our body and mind. In spite of his deep faith in Christ he felt intensely the negative inclinations in him. "I cannot understand my own behaviour. I fail to carry out the things I want to do. I find myself doing the things which I hate. I see the law of sin operating in my body, warring against the law that the mind dictates. What a wretched man I am, bonded to sin!" (Rom. 7:14-25). Honesty and humility to look deep into oneself in order to surrender to the saving grace of God is a prerequisite of the spiritual journey.

> *I see the law of sin*
> *operating in my body*
> Rom. 7:23

Meditation

Posture: I sit straight and relaxed; slowly I come to a bodily silence.

Breathing: With every in-breath I let the pranah energy flow upward along the spinal cord, and with every out-breath I let the energy flow from the heart chakra downward into the legs and the hands. (cfr, Ex. II. 2)

Recollection: I become aware of something that blocks the inner process in me, a *thorn in the flesh*: a negative inclination / a compulsive pattern of behaviour / an inordinate attachment / an unforgiving attitude / ...I face it without evoking guilt feeling or despair, and take it as an inner *virus* that blocks access to divine life in me

Inner word: Honestly acknowledging my existential weakness I dwell on the word: *I do the thing that I do not want* (Rom. 7:15).

VI.2. God in Flesh

"God wants everyone to be saved" (I. Tim. 2:4). Since the inner reason and the covenantal Law were unable to save humans from bondage to sinfulness and death, God entered human history in a most radical way. "God has done what the Law, being weakened by the flesh, could not do: God sent his own Son in the likeness of sinful flesh and condemned sin in the flesh" (Rom. 8:3). For Paul, Jesus Christ is not just a prophet who teaches the Law in a new way, but God´s self-gift. God entered the human body in a real sense and 'broke down the dividing wall of hostility caused by the Law' (Eph. 3:14); the Divine unfolded its compassionate face within history and united the estranged ones to a holy community (Gal. 3:28). No human being can redeem humans from the shackles of sin and transform human life to the divine life; only God can do that. God did this by giving himself, by sending his Son. "In the fullness of time God sent his Son, born of a woman, born a subject to the Law, to redeem us from subjugation to the Law to the freedom of the children of God" (Gal. 4:4-5)

In the death and resurrection of Jesus Paul sees the redemptive act of God. Through his suffering Jesus transformed human suffering (II Cor. 7:9- 10); through his death Jesus broke the devastating power of death (I Cor. 15:55); through his resurrection Jesus raised us to divine communion (Rom. 6:5); through his love Jesus conquered sin and gave us access to divine mercy (II Cor. 1:3-5). God reconciled the estranged world to himself (II Cor. 5:18-19). The divine atonement for human sinfulness is an act of infinite love. "Genuine love demands that one is prepared to die for the cause that one loves" (Mahatma Gandhi). "What proves that God loves us is that Christ died for us while we were still sinners" (Rom. 5:10).

The redemptive act of God in Jesus Christ is not just an event of the past, but the salvific process that takes place in the present, in the eternal *now*. Our life is a constant process of death to the sinful life and resurrection to the new life in God (Rom. 6:1-11). The spiritual journey is a constant movement from the old to the new, a transition from clinging on to the ego to openness to the Spirit. In this struggle faith in Christ endows us with hope and courage to move ahead in spite of the threat of sin and fear of death coming from the *flesh*. This was the dynamics of the life of Paul: "I forget the past and strain ahead for what is still to come, to capture the prize for which Christ has captured me" (Phil. 3:11-13). This is the new life in Christ.

We have a Saviour
who went through the struggles
which we face
Hebr. 4:15

Meditation

Posture: I sit straight and relaxed; slowly I come to a bodily silence.

Breathing: With every in-breath I let the pranah energy flow upward along the spinal cord, and with every out-breath I let the energy flow from the heart chakra downward into the legs and the hands. (see Ex. II. 2)

Recollection: With trust and surrender I look intently at the face of the Crucified Christ. If it is a help I keep a crucifix before me, or else I fix attention on the inner image of the crucified Lord. I let the form of the crucified God affect me deeply.

Inner word: I dwell on the words: *Through Christ God reconciled the estranged world to himself* (II Cor. 5:18-19).

VI.3. Life in Christ

The entire theology of Paul could be summarised in one key phrase: *in Christ*. More than 200 times this phrase appears in his Letters. The transition from the old to the new ultimately means that our life evolves in Christ. "If anyone is in Christ, she / he is a new creation. The old is gone; behold, all things have become new" (II Cor. 5:16). (**Read the following reflections in polarity to the numbers in VI. 1**)

1. *God* created the human person in his image and likeness. With the entry of sin this image was tarnished. Human life got alienated from the divine source. But in diverse ways God spoke to human hearts through sages and prophets and guided human life back to the Divine. (Heb. 1:1)

2. In the fullness of time God revealed himself in an embodied way in *Jesus Christ*. "Christ is the end of the Law" (Rom. 10:4). He was born into the *flesh* with all its frailty and fragility. But 'in the body of Christ God condemned sin' (Rom. 8:3) and manifested the *power* of God (I Cor. 1:24). Through Christ the 'love of God has been poured into our hearts by the *Spirit*' (Rom. 5:5).

3. The divine Spirit transforms our life to the new life in Christ. "If the Spirit of him who raised Jesus from the dead is living in us, then he who raised Jesus from the dead will give life to our mortal bodies through the Spirit" (Rom. 8:11). Participation in divine life is a *grace*. "Sin has no more dominion over you for you are not under Law, but under grace" (Rom. 6:14).

4. Christ has made us *free* from bondage to sin (Gal. 5:1). "The law of the Spirit of life in Christ Jesus has set us free from the law of sin and death" (Rom. 8:2). It is freedom from 'life according to the flesh' and freedom unto 'life according to the Spirit' (Rom. 8:5-9). What motivates active life is not working according to the Law, but *faith* in the abiding power of the Spirit of Christ (Eph. 3:17).

5. Since the 'Spirit makes us daughters and sons of God' (Rom. 8:6), we live with joy (Phil. 4:4) and work with *love* (Gal. 5:13-14), for we belong to God's family.

6. The death of Christ has initiated us to new *life*. "We are dead to sin and alive for God in Christ Jesus" (Rom. 6:11). With this the transition from the old to the new reaches the goal: "The wage of sin is death; the gift of God is eternal life in Christ Jesus" (Rom. 6:23).

For Paul, Jesus is not just a man of the past, but the divine presence here and now. What God has given to humanity in the person of Jesus is 'life in Christ' in the *now*. "Our life is hidden in Christ" (Col. 3:3). "We grow in Christ" (Eph. 3:16). "We mature into the fullness of Christ" (Eph. 4:13). "Christ is our life" (Phil. 1:20). "Christ is the fulfilment of our life" (Col. 2:10).

> *I live,*
>
> *not I,*
>
> *but Christ lives in me.*
>
> Gal. 2:20

Meditation

Posture: I sit straight and relaxed; slowly I come to a bodily silence.

Breathing: With every in-breath I let the pranah energy flow upward along the spinal cord, and with every out-breath I let the energy flow from the heart chakra downward into the legs and the hands. (see Ex. II. 2)

Inner image: I sit like a fountain. I feel that a fountain opens up at the vital centre of my body. In it I feel the living presence of Christ. (see Ex. IV. 4)

Recollection: Christ is God-within-me, God-with-me (*Emmanuel*). The life of Christ unfolds in me like a living fountain. My life evolves in this Christic process.

Inner word: With every breath I repeat the refrain of Paul, *in Christ*, and let the consciousness of the living Christ unfold in me. Or else, I chant the name of Jesus evoking the Christ consciousness (see Ex. III. 2)

VI.4. Life in the Spirit

In Paul's vision, life in Christ is effectively life in the Spirit. "The Lord is Spirit, and where the Spirit of the Lord is, there is freedom" (II Cor. 3:17). Christ is present to us in the Spirit; we are present to Christ through the Spirit. It is the Spirit that binds our life to divine life in Christ: "Everyone who is joined to the Lord is one Spirit with him" (I Cor. 6:17). And it is the Spirit that deepens our consciousness to a divine perception: "The Spirit reaches the depth of God. We have received the divine Spirit that helps us perceive the gifts of God" (I Cor. 2:10-12).

The Spirit abides in us. From within our hearts the Spirit cries out, *Abba*, Father (Gal. 4:6), enabling us to call God *Abba*, Father (Rom. 8:15). It is a continuous process of grace by which we realise that we are 'daughters and sons of God, heirs of God and coheirs of Christ' (Rom. 8:15-17). With this the Spirit liberates us from the fear of being slaves unto the freedom of being children of God. (Rom. 8:14-15). The abiding presence of the Spirit makes our body to the 'temple of the Spirit' (I Cor. 6:19), our heart to a fountain of the Spirit (Rom. 5:5), our communities to a dwelling-place of God (Eph. 2:22).

We abide in the Spirit. "We live in the Spirit and we walk in the Spirit" (Gal. 5:25). Our actions come from the inner movements of the divine Spirit. (Gal. 5:16). If so, there is no danger of falling back to the *old* ways of life (Gal. 5:13). Rather, we live in the constant awareness that the Spirit is renewing our life to the *new* life in God. This brings a divine quality to our life endowing it with the fruits of the Spirit (Gal. 5:22).

The Spirit transforms our social life to a *Spirit*ual community. The dynamic elements of this process are the charisms which the *one* Spirit distributes for the liberation of the person and for the coherence of the community (I Cor. 12:4-11). The Spirit 'breaks down the walls' (Eph. 2:14), which divide humans on the basis of religion and culture, belief and heritage (I Cor. 12:13). "There are no more distinctions between Jew and Greek, slave and master, male and female; all are one in Christ" (Gal. 3:28).

Our consciousness is deepened to perceive the movements of the Spirit in the divine depth of the *now*. Faith gives us the alertness to ask constantly: what is the Spirit telling me at this moment? With this search one discerns the interior movements of the Spirit in dialogue with the *Spirit*ual community.

Journey with the Spirit
Gal. 5:25

Meditation

Posture: I sit straight and relaxed; slowly I come to a bodily silence.

Breathing: With every in-breath I let the pranah energy flow upward along the spinal cord, and with every out-breath I let the energy flow from the heart chakra downward into the legs and the hands. (see Ex. II. 2)

Inner image: I sit like a fountain. I feel that a fountain opens up at the vital centre of my body and its life-giving water streams through my entire body. In it I feel the life-giving presence of the divine Spirit rising in me like a powerful fountain energising the whole being. With every in-breath I feel how the fountain is nourished by the divine springs; in every out-breath I feel how the stream of the divine Spirit percolates in me. (see Ex. IV. 5)

Recollection: The Spirit of Christ permeates my being. The Spirit transforms my life into the new life in Christ. The Spirit makes me transparent to the divine stream of life and light.

Inner word: I listen inwardly to what the Spirit is telling me here and now, in the divine depth of the present moment. Or else, I tune myself to the groaning of the Spirit by repeating the invocation *Abba*...

VI.5. The Divine Life

Paul speaks of two levels of consciousness: the one centred on the flesh (*sarkikos*) and the other deepened by the Spirit (*pneumatikos*): "The carnal mind is at enmity with God, because it cannot submit to God's law. But we are in the Spirit because we realise that the Spirit of Christ dwells in us" (Rom. 8:7-9). Correspondingly there are two ways of life: led by the interests of the flesh or guided by the movements of the Spirit (Gal. 5:18-22).

With the transference of the centre from flesh to Spirit, with the transition from the old to the new, one realizes that one is deeply united with God through Christ in the Spirit. Human consciousness is elevated to the perception of participation in the divine life: to the realization that we are divine. "Everyone who is joined to the Lord is one Spirit with him" (I Cor. 6:17). "We live the life of Christ" (Gal. 2:20), "life in Christ" (Col. 3:3), "life unto Christ" (Eph. 4:13). The reality of Christ unfolds in us (Eph. 3:17), the glory of Chris shines through us (II Cor. 3:18), the love of Christ motivates us (II Cor. 5:14). "For me to live is Christ!" – exclaimed Paul (Phil. 1:21).

Here the relation to Christ evolves not just at the inter-personal level, but at a deeper trans-personal level; it is not merely a matter of devotion *to* Christ, but a mystical experience of life *in* Christ. Here Christ is much more the subject of experience than a mere object of veneration. "It is no longer I who live, but Christ lives in me" (Gal. 2:20). Christ becomes the true subject of our life and work. We find ourselves in the process of being transformed by the Spirit of Christ. "Christ takes shape in us through the Holy Spirit who reinstates the divinity in us." (Cyril of Alexandria, PG.75,1088). The realization of the divinization of the human (*theosis*) in the divine depth of the *now* is the deepest mystical experience of Christian faith.

The outcome of this realization is a life of genuine love and compassion. "Serve one another in works of love" (Gal. 5:13) – Paul admonishes the community. When we realise that we are parts of the body of Christ, love binds the hearts (Col. 3:14-15). What our participation in the divine life means to us is expressed in the following words: "May Christ dwell in your hearts through faith. Being rooted and grounded in love, may you comprehend with all the saints the breadth and the length, the height and the depth until knowing the love of Christ, which is beyond all knowledge, you are filled with the utter fullness of God" (Eph. 3:17-19).

For me life is Christ
Phil. 1:21

Meditation

Posture: I sit straight and relaxed; slowly I come to a bodily silence.

Breathing: With every in-breath I let the pranah energy flow upward along the spinal cord, and with every out-breath I let the energy flow from the heart chakra downward into the legs and the hands (see Ex. II. 2).

Inner image: I take in the image of a crystal kept in sunlight. Every molecule of the crystal is brightened up by the beams of light

Recollection: Christ is the divine beam of light shining through me. I feel how the Spirit enlightens my consciousness to a Christic consciousness. I feel the utter transparency to the divine presence in me. The divine Light brightens up every bit of my being.

Inner word: I dwell on the process indicated in the words: *that we may be filled with the utter fullness of God* (Eph. 3:19).

7. The Seed

The inner spiritual journey is a process of holistic transformation. There is a death to the ego-fixation and rising to the true self-awareness. An archetype for this transition is the process that a seed goes through. Jesus uses this imagery to describe his being-with-us. (Jn. 12, 24). As a grain of wheat Jesus lived in our midst, went through the suffering of being thrown on the ground: the sheath of the ego-will broke and he became totally one with the divine ground. From there he rose up as an abiding source of new life. This is not just an event of the past; this is the way *God is with us* here and now: participating in our suffering and creating a new life.

In this series of meditations we shall pursue the evolutionary process of a seed. It is important to identify ourselves with the seed that goes through the process of being thrown into the earth, broken and transformed. The sequence of the *inner words* is taken from the meditation method developed by Karlfried Graf Dürckheim. (Der Alltag als Übung, Hans Huber, Bern, 1972)

We shall be taking the great Christian mystic **Meister Eckhart** (1260-1328) as our guide in this series of meditations. Trained as a theologian in the Dominican Order Eckhart became a spiritual master and inspiring preacher in the latter part of his life (1311-1328). He addressed mostly lay women and men who were passionately searching a mystical way of experiencing the Divine. He spoke out of an inner inspiration, and the listeners used to take down notes of his sermons. These notes were later located, edited and published. We shall use extracts from two recent editions of these collections in the reflections.

M. = Mieth, Dietmar, Meister Eckhart, Einheit im Sein und Wirken, (Selections of Eckhart's Sermons), Piper, Munich, 1991 (translation mine)

Q. = Quint, Josef, Meister Eckhart, Deutsche Predigte und Traktate, (Collected Sermons of Eckhart), Diogenes, Munich, 1979 (translation mine)

The Exercises:

Closely following the process of the seed we shall take five steps:

1. From the narrow ego-fixation I let myself go
2. Onto the divine ground I let myself fall
3. With the divine ground I let me become one
4. Merging into the divine stream of life I let me become new
5. Waking to the divine sunlight I grow in harmony with all.

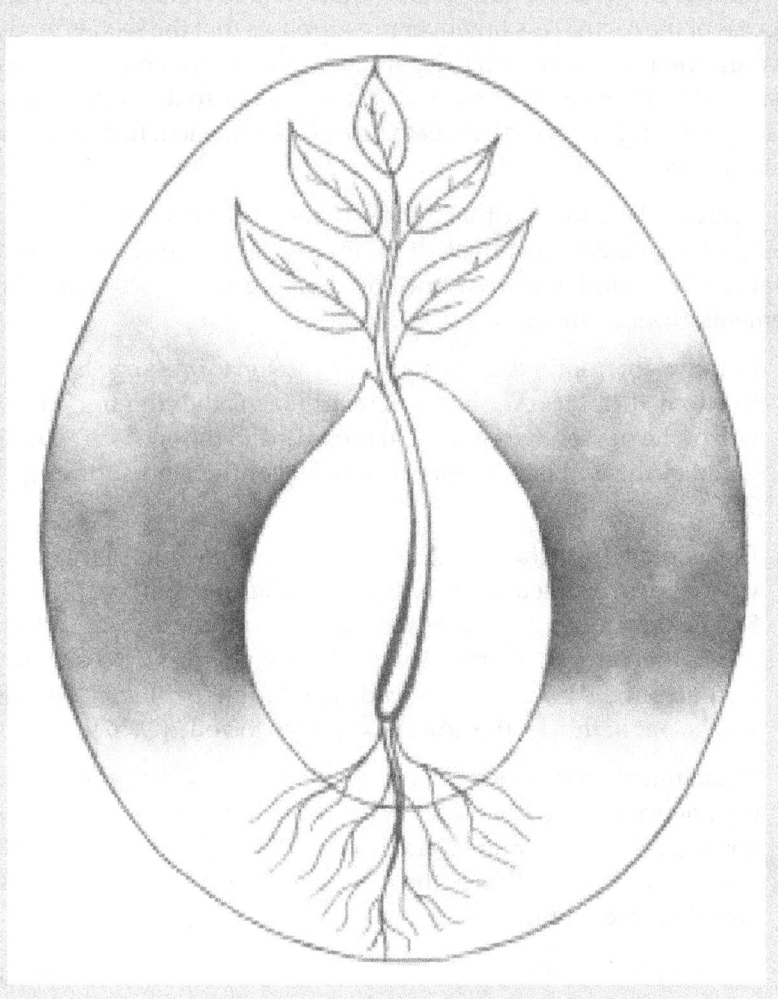

VII.1. Detachment

The seed has two options: either to remain in the container and end up on the frying pan, or to let itself be thrown into the earth and evolve into a plant. The second path of evolution means that the one seed becomes the mother of hundreds of seeds. It surrenders itself to the life-bearing process of the earth. This however presupposes that the seed is ready to give up the provisional security it has in the warm container totally insulated from the rest of creation. "The seed has to die" (Jn. 12, 24). It has to go through a process of death to itself, detachment from its present state of being.

This is where the spiritual transformation in us begins. Eckhart calls it *Abgeschiedenheit* (detachment). It means freedom from ego-fixation and total readiness to be thrown into the divine ground. There are three elements in detachment:

1. Detachment from ego: "Any form of adhesion to one's ego takes away freedom" (M. 116). With this Eckhart means the clinging on to the will of the possessive ego. What binds one to the ego is greed. "The greed of the will is the root cause of all conflict and suffering" (Q. 91).

2. Detachment from the world: "To be empty of creatures is to be filled with God; to be filled with God means to be empty of creatures" (M. 88). Eckhart does not advocate a flight from the world, rather he insists that one can liberatively get engaged in the world only if one is free from the possessive attitude in relation to things. "The more you go out of things, the more God comes to you" (Q. 57).

3. Detachment from God: "You have to let God go, if you want to experience the Divine" (M. 151). On the inner journey the seeker has to get rid of the names and images in which he conceives God. "Where an image is born, the Divine gives way; where the image vanishes, the Divine enters" (M. 126).

Eckhart is one of the greatest mystics of the apophatic tradition. The Divine is far beyond the *God* – this is a refrain in his sermons. Let the Divine be the Divine (M. 126), let creatures be creatures (M. 313), and let the ego wake to the deeper self (M. 123). Eckhart used to tell spiritual seekers: realise who you are, become what you are, go on your way!

Remove the rust in you,
and you will discover
the self glittering
from within.

Eckhart, M. 103

Meditation

Posture: I sit straight and relaxed; slowly I come to a bodily silence.

Breathing: With every in-breath I let the pranah energy flow upward along the spinal cord, and with every out-breath I let the energy flow from the heart chakra downward into the legs and the hands. (see Ex. II. 4)

Recollection: I become aware of some of the attachments which bind me to the possessive ego and block the inner process.

Inner image: I visualise the image of a seed that is being taken out of the container and thrown into the earth. I feel into the seed and sense its fear and anxiety, its courage and confidence: its basic readiness to give up the provisional identity.

Inner word: As the breathing takes place without the assertion of my ego-will, I feel with every out-breath an inner detachment from the ego-fixation. At the beginning of every out-breath I say interiorly: *let go.* With that I feel a certain inner freedom growing in me: surrender to the work of the Spirit in me.

VII.2. The Ground of Being

The seed allows itself be thrown into the earth. There is a moment of fear and anxiety here. The small seed does not know where it is falling. It is like a leap into the abysmal depth of reality. The earth affectionately embraces it, takes it to her womb. The sheath of the seed now breaks. It is a process of suffering: the cover that till now assured identity to the seed falls off. The little seed lies denuded and lonely within the earth. The life-giving energy stream of the earth absorbs it and a process of transformation sets is. A joyful confidence wakes up in the little seed: I cannot fall deeper than into the lap of the mother earth from which I am born. It is a home-coming for the seed, a ray of hope for a new identity.

On the inner spiritual journey one has to detach oneself from the ego-fixation and let fall. To describe the bearing and nourishing divine presence into which one falls Eckhart uses the image *Seinsgrund*: the ground of being. "Here one stands on the ground, on the basis, in the stream, at the well-springs of the Divine" (M. 193). It is not just surrender to a personal God before us, but letting oneself fall into the transpersonal divine ground within us. Eckhart consistently makes a distinction between the *God* and the *Godhead* (*der Gott - die Gottheit*). (I prefer to use the substantive *the Divine* instead of *Godhead*). The *God* is the personal form that we conceive; the *Divine* is the transpersonal ground that we can experience. "God and the Divine are distinct. God appears when the creatures cry out, *God*. But as I reached the ground of being, the basis, the inner stream, the well-springs, I realised: the *God* vanishes" (M. 193).

At the deeper levels of mystical introspection one has to leave behind all names and forms of God. "Even the smallest image of God blocks your access to the Divine" (M. 126). Eckhart insists that all the personified forms of the Divine, which may have comfortably accompanied the seeker at the mental level, have to be transcended. One has to sink `into the hidden darkness of the eternal divinity´ (M. 141), `into the abysmal depth of the divine ocean' (M. 131), `into the stillness of the inner desert' (M. 145). With the great apophatic mystics Eckhart demands that one has to go through this agonising process of Godlessness (M. 154) if one wants to see the true divine light within. "Do you want to experience God as the Divine? Then you have to let your knowing turn to unknowing, to the total forgetting of your ego-self and all beings" (M. 173).

It is a tremendous experience of being confronted with the 'nothingness' of being in relation to the fullness of the Divine. The feeling of nothingness comes through a total detachment from mental constructs and through the sense of the utter incomprehensibility of the divine ground. It is a liberative experience of self-emptying (*kenosis*) that makes space for the divine Spirit to enter and deepen the consciousness.

> *Go back to the divine ground*
> *from where you came forth.*
>
> Eckhart, M. 170

Meditation

Posture: I sit straight and relaxed, preferably on the floor. I feel how I am deeply grounded on the mother earth. (see Ex. I. 2)

Breathing: With every in-breath I let the pranah energy flow upward along the spinal cord, and with every out-breath I let the energy flow from the heart chakra downward into the legs and the hands. (see Ex. II. 4)

Inner image: I take in the image of a seed that falls on the earth. I feel how the seed senses itself while being taken in by the earth.

Recollection: I put aside all personified names and forms of God and become aware of the Divine as the ground of being: that from which I am born, that through which I live, and that unto which I return.

Inner word: With every breath I place myself on the divine ground. Towards the end of every out-breath I say interiorly *let fall*. With that I feel how I am taken in by the divine ground and prepared for a Spirit-generated process of growth.

VII.3. The Dynamic Oneness

The seed is absorbed by the earth. The seed becomes one with the mother earth. Its being is not annihilated but transformed; its life is not destroyed but recreated. The earth into which it falls is not inert matter, but the matrix of life-giving energies. The little seed is taken into the enlivening streams of the mother earth.

When the sheath of the ego-self is removed, then the true self is taken in by the divine Self and it becomes one with the divine ground. "Here the divine ground is my ground, and my ground is the divine ground" (M. 124). Mystics across the centuries and religions affirm that only in oneness with the Divine shall we experience the Divine. "In oneness you find the Divine. Anyone who longs to find the Divine must become one with the Divine" (M. 105). The ultimate basis for this mystical union is that `the Divine is ONE in all its purity and simplicity, free of names and forms´ (M. 120). "All that is in the Divine is ONE, and no one can say anything about it" (M. 193). Hence to attain the divine reality one has to merge into the Divine, as the seed merges into the earth (Q.355).

But the Divine as the ONE does not mean a static one-ness (*unus*), rather the Divine is a dynamic unity (*unum*) (Thomas Aquinas, ST I.31.2.ad 4). The divine ground is not an inert entity but a life-giving process. From a static thing no life can evolve; from an impersonal source no love can emerge. The inner-divine dynamics of life and love is represented in the Christian perception of Father-Son-Spirit. Eckhart gives a mystical interpretation to the mystery of the Trinity: "In this ONE, in the innermost divine ground, the Father gives birth to the Son, and the Spirit unfolds as the Blossoming" (M. 126). "The Father gives birth to the Son into the innermost core of the Spirit" (M. 124).

Eckhart cautions on designating Father-Son-Spirit as three persons. The image of *persona* comes from the dualistic mental understanding. This cannot reach out to the depth of the Divine. "The divine ONE is without forms and attributes. If *God* were to gaze into it, that would cost him all his divine names and personal attributes. All these must stay outside" (M. 120). Mystical introspection takes us to the perception of the trans-personal mystery of the Divine: to the experience of the Divine as the ultimate source of life and *subject* of our being. It is out of this depth of experience that Jesus lived and worked; it is to this depth that we are called. Eckhart accompanies the seekers to this inner realm. There we realise that our life evolves not before God, but within the Divine:

within the inner-trinitarian process of Life. To this realisation we come when we are fully present to the present moment. Eternity is the divine depth of the *now*. (M. 118).

> *One with the ONE,*
> *one from the ONE,*
> *eternally one in the ONE-*
>
> Eckhart, M. 110

Meditation

Posture: I sit straight and relaxed. I feel the deep oneness with the earth: my body is earth; the earth is my body. (see Ex. I. 2)

Breathing: With every breath I feel the upward stream of prana along the spinal cord and the downward stream into the entire body. I sense how the pranah energy becomes one with my body. (see Ex. II. 4)

Inner Image: I take in the image of the seed that falls into the earth and becomes one with the earth. I feel with the process of the seed.

Recollection: I sense a deep oneness with the divine ground: God is not just a personal object before me, but the nourishing subject within me.

Inner word: As every out-breath comes to an end there is a pause for a moment. In the stillness of this pause I say interiorly *be one*.

VII.4. Birth of God in the Soul

The seed is absorbed by the earth and brought into the life-giving streams of the earth. Its being is not destroyed, but its life is transformed. It is led to a new identity. From a lonely state of insulation from the rest of creation it is now brought into integration with all. The sprout gradually becomes a mother of hundreds of seeds. The earth gives birth to a new plant; in fact the earth gives birth to herself through the plant. In and through the plant the earth blossoms forth and bears fruit. The earth is the vibrant subject.

The new life that emerges in the seed is a symbol of what happens in the human self under the impact of the indwelling Spirit. Eckhart calls it 'the birth of God in the soul'. Inserted to the inner-trinitarian process we are constantly being born anew in the Divine, and God gives birth to himself in us. "The Father gives birth to the Son in me and he gives birth to me as well. The Father gives birth to me as his son/daughter. In fact he gives birth to himself as me: my being and nature is divine. From the deepest divine well-springs I spring forth in the divine Spirit. There is only *one* life, *one* being, *one* work" (Q. 185). In a graced state of mystical intuition we could say: we are divine.

The plant that is born out of the mother earth nourishes the earth in return. The plant bears seeds, and seeds merge into the earth and bear further plants. Following this cyclic imagery Eckhart says: born of the Divine we give birth to God. "The Father gives birth to the Son into the depth of the soul. In the same process, in which the Father bears the Son into me, I bear him back to the Father" (M. 138). We are called not only to be the daughters / sons of God, but also mothers of God. "I give birth to the One who gives birth to me!" (M. 137). Divine life blossoms forth through us. In a compassionate word, in an act of mercy, in a smile that brings joy, for instance, God is born in our midst.

With the great Church Fathers like Gregory of Nyssa and Augustine Eckhart reflects on the mystical sense of Incarnation. "God wants to be born through every human soul" (M. 134). Through total detachment we make our true self receptive to the Divine; this is the state of being a *virgin*. Through the realization of what we truly are we grow to maturity in spiritual life; this is the process of becoming a *woman*. Then the divine Spirit impregnates the soul with the power of the divine Word; thus the soul becomes *mother*. "It is more precious to God to be born spiritually from every such virgin, from every good soul, than that he was bodily born of Mary" (M. 134). Christian faith enables us to recognize this process in Jesus Christ. Faith is an invitation to participation in the divinisation of the human. It is an intuitive experience of total transparency to the Divine within, a mystical experience of union with the divine ground: the Divine is the true subject of our life.

> God wants to be
>
> fruit-bearing
>
> in every person.
>
> Eckhart, M. 115

Meditation

Posture: I sit straight and relaxed. I feel in the body the nourishing power of the earth. (see Ex. I. 2)

Breathing: With every breath I feel the upward stream of pranah along the spinal cord and the downward stream into the entire body. I sense how every breath revitalises my body. (see Ex. II. 4)

Inner image: I take in the image of the seed that merges into the earth enabling a new sprout come forth from the seed. I sense how the earth gives birth to herself through the sprout.

Recollection: The divine Spirit impregnates my soul: I am being born into divine life; God is being born in and through me. The divine Self unfolds through my self.

Inner word: With every in-breath I recall interiorly: *renewed*.

VII.5. Universal Theophany

The seed sprouts forth and evolves into a plant. With the sprouting the seed attains a new identity. From isolation it is led to integration with all. The sun energy draws it out from the womb of the earth; the breath energy vitalises every cell. The little plant acquires new shapes and fresh colours. Hundreds of flowers and seed-bearing fruits evolve. The plant grows in harmony with the rest of creation.

A similar process takes place in our spiritual life too. The Divine unfolds in and through us. This theonomous process integrates our true self to the rest of creation: we live in harmony with every person, with everything else. We feel like branches of a divine tree, deeply rooted in the divine ground and intimately related to all others.

The spiritual vision of Eckhart leads to an experience of this cosmic theophany. "One sees God in all, and everything in God" (M. 272). "One tastes God in all things" (M. 191). "One perceives the Divine in all beings" (M. 106). The entire world is perceived as divine milieu, as sacred space. "God works as the Indweller (*Innerster*) from within the core of all beings and unto the core of all things" (M. 311). The entire cosmos is seen within the inner-trinitarian process of life. "Everything is perceived as new, good, pure, clear and sacred in as much as everything is oriented towards God and returns to God"(M. 313).

For this integral spiritual vision one has to deepen one's consciousness. Eckhart makes a distinction between two levels of perception: exterior and interior, mental and intuitive. "To my exterior man all creatures taste like creatures only. My interior man does not taste things as creatures but rather as a gift of God. My innermost man, however, does not taste a creature as God's gift, but rather as something eternal" (M. 192). Engagement in the world with this mystical consciousness renders a new quality to life. "One should not flee from the things of this world to a place of seclusion; rather perceive them anew from within the inner solitude. One will then be able to break through the surface level of things and discover the Divine deep within the recess of them and make the things transmit the divine Light" (Q. 61). "We bring all things in their spiritual being unto our consciousness, so that they are all *one* in us" (M. 193).

Compassion, Eckhart says, is the characteristic of a person who 'does the works from within the innermost ground of being' (M. 125). "The greatest work of God is compassion, for God's very nature is compassion" (M. 130). Hence the one who lives and acts with a divine subject-consciousness will be primarily a compassionate person. "Love embraces the goodness of God; knowledge comprehends the truth of God. But compassion attains the Divine in its very being. Hence compassion is nobler than love and knowledge" (M, 131). Blessed are the compassionate, Jesus proclaimed. (Mt. 5: 7).

> *God shines forth in all things,*
> *for in all things*
> *you see nothing but God.*
> Eckhart, M. 179

Meditation

Posture: I sit straight and relaxed, preferably on the floor. I feel the deep oneness with the earth. (see Ex. I. 2)

Breathing: With every breath I feel the percolation of pranah in my body and the deep oneness with all beings. I breathe through all beings, and they breathe through me. (see Ex. II. 5)

Inner image: I take in the image of the seed that has now grown to a plant. I feel how the plant senses its deep rootedness in the earth and its intimate relatedness with all beings around.

Recollection: I sense the divine presence permeating the universe: God in all and all in God. In this stream of the divine energy I am integrated with all beings. All things are branches of one another on the divine Tree.

Inner word: Gratefully paying attention to breathing I repeat: *the breath of God breathes through me and through all.*

8. The Master

One encounters the divine master on the inner spiritual journey. The divine master meets the seeker not from outside, but from the inner sacred space, not as someone who just lived in the past, but as the divine Saviour who is present in the *eternal now*. One surrenders oneself in freedom and trust to the divine master, who in turn accompanies the human seeker to the deepest experience of oneness with the Divine. This is in fact a universal liberative experience described in most Holy Scriptures and spiritual classics. In this series of meditations we shall pursue the path delineated in the **Bhagavad Gita.**

The Gita, composed around 300 BCE, is a Holy Book of the Hindu heritage. As a spiritual classic it is a mystical poem that describes the dialogue between a human person that seeks God and the God that loves the humans. The text in fact 'articulates the perennial dialogue that takes place in the heart of every human person' (Mahatma Gandhi). Hence the Gita can be read beyond the boundaries of religions and cultures. The reader has to identify himself with Arjuna, the human seeker (*sādhaka*) of the Gita, and listen to the divine Word from the Sri Bhagavān, the inner divine master. *Sri Bhagavān* is a term that connotes God's gracious presence (*bhaj* = to share; *bhagavān* = the Lord who shares himself with us). In this sense each sadhaka could more or less discover in the Sri Bhagavān of the Gita the Lord according to one's religious heritage. Spiritual integration process evolves through a threefold path: (i) Bhakti: surrender oneself totally in love to the divine master. (ii) Jnāna: experience the unity with the Divine within oneself and in the cosmos. (iii) Karma: commit oneself to the divine work of integrating the world.

The Exercises:

The five meditations of this series take the seeker (*sādhaka*) step by step along this threefold path of spiritual integration.
1. I surrender myself totally to the divine master within me (*bhakti*).
2. I feel how I am slowly led to a deep experience of indwelling in the Divine.
3. I experience how my true self is united with the divine Self. (*jnāna*).
4. I look at the world as a sacred space wherein the divine Spirit is at work.
5. I realize that through works I participate in the divine work of dharma (*karma*).

Numbers in brackets refer to chapter and verse of the Bhagavad Gita

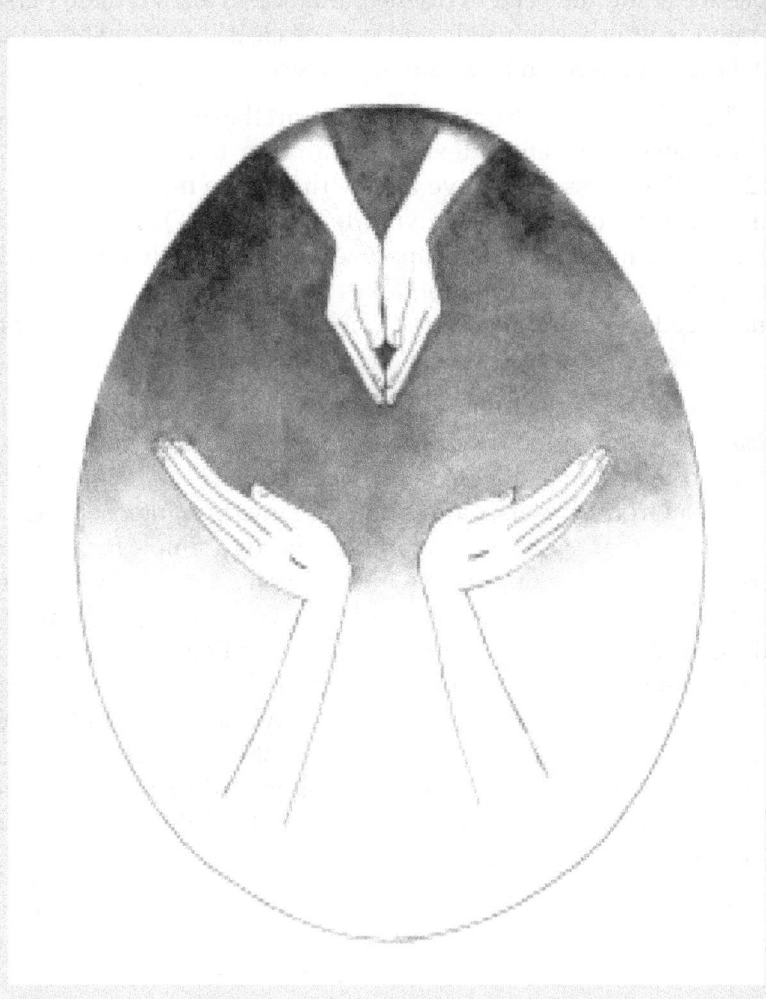

VIII.1. The Surrender

A total self-surrender to the inner divine master is the beginning of spiritual transformation. The sadhaka becomes aware of his / her present inner situation and frankly acknowledges the inner helplessness and the need of divine guidance. "I am a broken person; my mind is utterly confused; I do not see clearly what I should do" (2:7). Facing a crisis can be a salutary experience.

The sadhaka hears from within the heart the divine master's voice that resonates in the entire text: "You are dear to me!" (18:64; 4:3,11; 12:12-20). This message of love instils trust in the human soul: "I am your disciple; I take refuge in you: teach me" (2:7). With this self-surrender the human creates a space within for the Divine to act. The entire process of transformation takes place in the dialectic between human freedom (18:63) and divine grace (18:56). The human self opens itself in freedom and the divine Self manifests itself in grace.

The divine master invites the human sadhaka to total surrender in *bhakti*: "Fix your mind on me, open your psyche unto me, offer your buddhi to me, be my devotee and take refuge in me alone. I shall liberate you from all evils. Grieve not, for I love you intensely" (18:58, 65-66, 12:14). Bhakti is initially expressed through simple forms of self-offering: "Whosoever offers me with devotion a leaf or flower or fruit or water, that offering of a pure hearted soul I will accept" (9:26). And bhakti can take different channels: "In whatsoever way devotees come to me, in that way do I accept them" (4:11; 7:21). Hence bhakti is accessible to sadhakas of all grades of society and states of life: "Even people who are considered to be sinners or of inferior birth can reach me through bhakti" (9:30-32). They are all graced to hear the salvific message: "I shall not let my devotee perish" (9:31). Bhakti is the universal path of salvation.

How does bhakti become salvific? Through total inner self-surrender to the divine master one overcomes the fixation on the possessive ego (*ahamkāra*) and grows towards a liberative self-consciousness (*ātmabōdha*). It is greed (*kāma*) that causes the false identity feeling around the ego. "Kama is like an insatiable fire that devours everything; know it to be the enemy within you; slay this enemy, so hard to conquer!" (3:37, 39, 44). This is the enemy that is constantly alluded to in the Gita and hence the entire discourse refers to an *inner* warfare. The sadhaka should discern the destructive forms in which kama operates in his / her life: uncontrolled emotions (16:18), craving for political power (16:14), greed for material wealth (16:13), pride of being born in a higher caste (16:15), misuse of religious rituals for personal gains (16:17) - which all lead to the feeling that one is the *Lord of all* (16:14). Left to oneself one cannot surmount these negative forces built into the psyche (*chitta*) through the *gunas*. (18:58). The way to inner freedom is to surrender oneself to the divine master (18:62).

This is the first stage of bhakti.

> *Take refuge in Him with all your being;*
> *by the divine grace you will attain*
> *the eternal abode, the supreme peace.*
>
> Bh. Gita 18:62

Meditation

Posture: I sit straight and relaxed, preferably on the earth with both the hands laid open.

Breathing: With every in-breath I let the pranah energy flow upward along the spinal cord, and with every out-breath I let the energy flow from the heart chakra downward into the legs and the hands. Gradually I feel how the energy vibrations flow beyond my body to the world outside. The breath of God breathes through me. (see Ex. II. 5)

Inner image: I imagine that I am wandering through the dark paths of life. I become aware of something that deeply disturbs me. With deep trust I surrender myself unconditionally to the divine master. (The concrete name / form of the divine master will depend on the faith-heritage of the sadhaka). The divine master meets me not from outside, but from within the inner divine space. The encounter takes place in the divine space of the *heart*.

Inner word: With every breath I chant interiorly: śishyasté aham śādhi mām tvām prapannam (I am your disciple, teach me, I take refuge in you, Bh. Gita, 2:7)

VIII.2. The Indwelling

On the inner spiritual journey the divine master leads the human sadhaka to deeper levels of consciousness. The process begins with an inter-personal relationship between human person and God (bhakti). The human sadhaka surrenders himself / herself to the divine master. Gradually the relationship moves to the intra-personal and trans-personal levels of consciousness (jnāna). The human self finds itself not so much *before* God, as *within* the Divine. God as friend and master is here experienced as the divine ground of being and fountain of life within. The divine presence unfolds from the depth of being.

At a deeper stage of the inner journey the sadhaka of the Gita cries out: "Lord I want to see your true form" (11:3). The universal human quest is articulated here. To this comes the reply from the depth of being: "With this your natural eye you cannot see me. A divine eye I shall bestow: now behold my divine mystery" (11:8). With the power of grace the Lord opens the divine eye that is imbedded in the buddhi. The Divine can be seen only in the divine light. An ardent quest, expressed in genuine self-surrender, is the way to get the inner eye enlightened. "Not by Vedic scholarship or ascetic practice, not by almsgiving or sacrificial rituals can you see me truly. Only by unswerving bhakti to me can you know me, see me and enter into me" (11:53-54).

The sadhaka grows in the mystical realisation of living *in* the Divine. "If your mind is fixed on me and your buddhi dwells in me, you will live in me" (12:8). "The one who worships me present in all beings lives in me, whatever be his / her mode of life" (6:31). Bhakti enables the soul to have a deep communion with the Divine. Through bhakti one `enters my abode´ (6:15), `comes close to me´ (9:28), `reaches me´ (10:10), `attains me´ (7, 23) and `lives in me´ (18: 55). In the light of divine grace the sadhaka realises that the true self is being transformed by divine love. "Those who worship me with genuine love, they are in me and I am in them" (9:29). Here God is experienced not so much as a person before us, but as the presence within us; God is not so much an object of veneration, but the subject of experience. The sadhaka realises that God is the true subject of his / her life and work. "I am the Self seated at the heart of all beings" (10:20). "I dwell in the hearts of all; from me come forth memory, clarity and dispelling of doubts" (15:15).

Experiencing the Divine as the true subject does not mean denial of human freedom. After the long discourse the divine Master tells the human sadhaka: "I have revealed to you the deepest divine secret; dwell on this wisdom and do as you decide" (18: 63). And immediately comes the assurance: whatever be the human response, the divine Love never fails (18:64).

This is the second stage of bhakti that grows into jnāna.

Those who worship me with genuine love,
they are in me
and I am in them.
Bh. Gita, 9:29.

Meditation

Posture: I sit straight and relaxed, preferably on the earth.

Breathing: With every in-breath I let the pranah energy flow upward along the spinal cord, and with every out-breath I let the energy flow from the heart chakra downward into the legs and the hands. Gradually I feel how the energy vibrations flow beyond my body to the world outside. The breath of God breathes through me. (see Ex. II. 5)

Inner image: I feel myself as a pot that is immersed in water: the pot is in water and water is in the pot. Like the pot I am immersed in the divine presence. Another helpful image could be that of the tree: the branches are in fact in the stem, and the stem is in the branches. I feel myself as a branch on the divine tree. I am in God and God is in me.

Inner word: With every in-breath I say interiorly: *you in me*; And with every out-breath I say: *I in you*. Or else, I go on repeating with every breath: *mayi tē, tēshuaham* (They are in me, I am in them, Bh. Gita, 9: 29)

VIII.3. The Oneness

In bhakti God is encountered as a personal thou; in jnana the Divine is intuited as the transpersonal Self. Bhakti motivates self-surrender; jnāna invites introspection. Though *prima facie* Bhagavad Gita may look like a bhakti text, there is a strong undercurrent of jnāna experience emerging from the Upanishadic heritage.

The deepening of consciousness following from an inter-personal encounter with God to the transpersonal experience of the divine Ground takes place primarily through meditation (*dhyāna*). The Sanskrit term suggests the journey (*yāna*) through the buddhi (*dhi*). In meditation the senses are controlled by the mind (6:24), the mind is fixed on the inner self (6:25), the psyche is brought to serenity (12:9), the buddhi is made steadfast (6:25), and the self is laid open to the Self (6:6). "Elevate the self by the Self!" (6:5) – this is the call to meditation. It is a process of getting the human self totally united (*yōga*) with the divine Self. Gita calls it *buddhi-yōgam*, since this one-ness is experienced through the buddhi (18:57). Ultimately it is a matter of divine grace: "To those who commune with me in love, to these well integrated souls *I grant buddhi-yōgam*, by which they attain me" (10:10).

When the light of the buddhi is illumined (10:11), when the eye of the buddhi is opened (11:8), the sadhaka "perceives the self in the Self through the Self" (6: 20; 13: 24). In the divine light one realises one's true self within the divine Self (13:17). This is an experience of immense bliss (6: 21) and inner freedom (3: 17). With this, one comes to the deepest realisation of what one foundationally is: I am divine! "One who is purified through the buddhi and self-restraint,...ever engaged in meditation,...freed from the possessive ego-fixation,...is destined to become divine" (*brahmabhuyāya*, 18:51-53). "And having been thus divinised, one perceives the Divine in all things; this is the supreme experience of communion" (18: 54).

Thus jnāna is the realisation of the divine dimension of one's true being. "I consider the jnani to be my very self" (7: 18). When through grace one comes to this realization one experiences the Divine as the true subject of one's being. Liberative action comes from a divine source (3:15). Human works can then be done in total surrender to the divine agency that energises and sanctifies human endeavour. "The one who does works without attachment, but having surrendered them all to the Divine, remains untouched by sin or impurity" (5:10). Jnana thus gives a new quality to life, a divine perspective on the world, an inner freedom in getting engaged in works.

This is the deepest *jnāna* that evolves into karma.

> *Freed from ego-fixation*
> *you are destined to*
> *be divinised.*
>
> Bh. Gita, 18:53

Meditation

Posture: I sit straight and relaxed.

Breathing: With every in-breath I let the pranah energy flow upward along the spinal cord, and with every out-breath I let the energy flow from the heart chakra downward into the legs and the hands. Gradually I feel how the energy vibrations flow beyond my body to the world outside. The breath of God breathes through me. (see Ex. II. 5)

Inner image: I take in an image that helps me to become aware of the deep oneness with the divine ground of being, to feel the utter transparency to the divine light. I identify myself, for instance, with a clear crystal through which beams of sunlight penetrate and brighten up every particle. Or, I feel myself like a piece of iron glowing in the furnace, totally consumed by the fire. Another image could be that of a drop of water merging into the ocean. I gratefully become aware of the divine dimension of my true self.

Inner word: With every breath I repeat: *ātmani ātmānam ātmanā paśysati* (see the self in the Self through the Self, Bh. Gita, 6:20)

VIII.4. The Cosmic Vision

Before moving to karma, it is important to pay attention to the cosmic dimension of jnana. With the inner eye, enlightened by divine light, one looks not only into the inner space, but to the world outside too. The consciousness that is focussed on the divine presence within is now laid open to the cosmic horizons. One sees the Divine everywhere. "The integrated person perceives the Self in all beings and all beings in the Self" (6:29). It is an intense experience of the universal theophany: the divine light shines through all (13:17), the divine presence pulsates in all beings (18:61), the divine life enlivens everything (7:8-11), and the divine sound vibrates in all (9:17). "I am the Self seated in the hearts of all beings. I am the beginning, the middle and the end of all" (10:20). "I am the light in the sun, in the moon and in fire, I am the power of fertility percolating the earth and nourishing the vegetation, I am the undying seed of all beings, I abide at the heart of all things" (15:12-13, 7:10, 15:15) . Only with a *divine eye* can one perceive this universal immanence of the Divine (11:8). God is the father and mother, the ground and abode, the way and goal, the friend and refuge, the origin and dissolution. (9:17-18).

The inner journey of the sadhaka began with an attitude of total self-surrender. The divine master deepened the consciousness and enlarged the vision.. "Who sees me everywhere and everything in me, with that person I am ever united" (6: 30). In this theonomous vision the entire universe is now perceived as the temple of the Lord, as the sacred space permeated by the divine master. "The one deeply united with me, worships me as present in all beings. Such a person lives and moves in me, whatever be his / her mode of living" (6:31). Every person, every thing communicates the power and presence of the Divine, for everything has its root in the divine ground (15:1). The entire universe is experienced as the body of the divine Lord (11:13). As parts of a body, as branches of a tree, everything is bound with everything else in the universal divine stream of life. (3:14-15). It is in this interconnectedness that life and activity get a divine quality.

Jnana is the realisation of the divine dimension of the cosmic reality. It is the realisation of the deep unity between the Divine, the cosmic and the human. It is not a matter of mental understanding but a mystical intuition into the deep oneness of reality. One experiences an inner transparency in which a deep sense of the ontic interconnectedness wakes up. One finds that one's true self has become the Self of all (*sarva bhūtātma bhūtātma*, 5: 7). Then one sees all things as reflections of one's own self (6: 32).

This cosmic experience of *jñāna* leads to karma.

> *God lives*
> *at the heart*
> *of all beings.*
>
> Bh. Gita, 15:15

Meditation

Posture: I sit straight and relaxed.

Breathing: With every in-breath I let the pranah energy flow upward along the spinal cord, and with every out-breath I let the energy flow from the heart chakra downward into the legs and the hands. Gradually I feel how the energy vibrations flow beyond my body to the world outside. The breath of God breathes through me. (see Ex. II. 5)

Inner word: With the repetition of OM I try to feel the divine vibrations in everything around me. Eventually I repeat a phrase that will awaken me to the experience of the divine immanence, e.g.: *sarva bhūtātma bhūtātmā* (my self has become the very Self of all, 5:7) *iśāvāsyamidam sarvam* (all this is permeated by the Lord, Isa Up. I)

VIII.5. The Solidarity

Bhakti as surrender is deepened by jnana as experience of the divine immanence. The consequence is karma: the sadhaka commits himself / herself to the divine work of integration (dharma). This is the active response to the perception of the divine immanence in all beings. With the inner eye of the enlightened buddhi one perceives the dynamic presence of the Divine in the world: God is engaged in bringing about the integral welfare of all beings; this motivates the sadhaka to work as an instrument in the hands of God in the promotion of dharma. Karma is human participation in the divine dharma.

Karma becomes liberative when it is done not from the ego-fixation (ahamkāra), but from a divine self-consciousness (ātmabōdha). "The ignorant ones act from attachment to their work; the wise persons act in freedom from greed" (3:25). "United in the divine ground one should engage in works without attachment (2: 48). Such a spiritual mode of work alone leads to integral liberation (4: 23). There is a twofold motivation for *karmayoga*: the welfare of humanity and the harmony of the universe.

What motivates the works of a sadhaka in social commitment is 'a passionate concern for the integral welfare of humanity' (*lokasamgraha*, 3:25). This regulates political involvement and economic interests (3:20; 15:13-16). The hallmark of a liberated person is 'compassion, kind-heartedness and friendliness' (12:13-14). When one sees the divine presence in all persons, one responds with equanimity respecting all: 'friends and foes' (12:18), 'dear ones and unpleasant ones' (6:9), 'low-caste and high-caste' (5:18).

There is also a concern of eco-harmony. The enlightened person looks at the entire universe as a cosmic web: deeply interconnected in the divine dynamics of life. All beings are revolving as if on a wheel energised by the divine hub. "Work arises from a divine source" (3:15). Humans participate in this divine work of cosmic harmony through *yajna*, self-sacrifice. Yajna is work done sacrificing the ego-fixation (4:23), work performed in the `spirit of service' (Mahatma Gandhi). "The Creator Lord created all beings binding them together in yajna. Hence we humans have to protect the powers of nature, and they in turn will take care of us; mutually nourishing each other we all attain prosperity. Instead, if we exploit the resources of nature we are thieves. Those who cook food only for themselves eat poison" (3:9-13).

Bhakti brings about integration within the person; jnāna deepens the consciousness and offers an integral vision of reality; karma leads to solidarity with others and concern for eco-harmony. All the three paths form an integral process of spiritual transformation open to believers of all religions. Being a mystical text Bhagavad Gita is a universal Scripture.

> *Works done*
> *in the sense of service alone*
> *leads to integration.*
> Bh. Gita, 4:23

Meditation

Posture: I sit straight and relaxed.

Breathing: Through conscious breathing I come to a deep bodily silence. I feel how the prana energy flows beyond the body and percolates through all beings. I sense the divine life-energy streaming through all. (see Ex. II. 5)

Inner image: I visualise that I am a branch on the cosmic divine Tree. I am deeply bonded to all other branches in the one stream of the vital sap. I recall a concrete form of my involvement in the world: in the family / profession / society. I perceive my work as an integral part of the divine work of bringing integral prosperity in the world. I become aware of the divine significance of my life and work. I look at everything with compassion.

Inner word: With every breath I repeat a word like *yogasthah kuru karmāni* (being united with the divine ground, do the works, Bh. Gita, 2: 48).

PART III
Graces of Silence

9. The Way

In spiritual life the way is already the goal: as we let ourselves be guided on the way of the divine Spirit, we are already at the goal of God experience. Our journey then evolves in a divine ambience. Constant alertness to the movements of the Spirit deep within us and around us is the dynamics of spiritual life. Thus one is already in the *energy field* of the Divine, in the process of realising the divine dimension of one's self. The God who deepens our consciousness within is the God who walks with us on the complex ways of daily life.

Three aspects of the divine presence are taken up in this series:
- the divine saviour walks with us on our way of suffering and on the way of creativity as well.
- the divine grace inserts our life to the divine life.
- the divine Spirit transforms the cosmos to a new creation.

In these five meditations we touch the heart of Christian spirituality: God is with us (*Emmanuel*). Faith in the crucified saviour reveals the God who is with us as the suffering God; faith in the risen Christ assures us that God is with us in our creative endeavours. The divine Spirit makes us participate in the divine Life and brings about a new creation. All this means that our life evolves in a divine process. God is not just before / above us; God is with us, within us. Christ is God-with-us, God-within-us. Christ is the ultimate subject of our being.

The Exercises:
1. I honestly acknowledge the shadows and sufferings on the path of my life.
2. Through my faith in the crucified Jesus I realise that Christ walks with me on the path of my suffering.
3. In the light of my faith in the risen Christ I experience that Christ recreates my life into a new life.
4. In deep silence I experience that my life is participation in the divine Life through grace.
5. In deep spiritual communion with all beings I realise that my work is participation in the divine work of the New Creation.

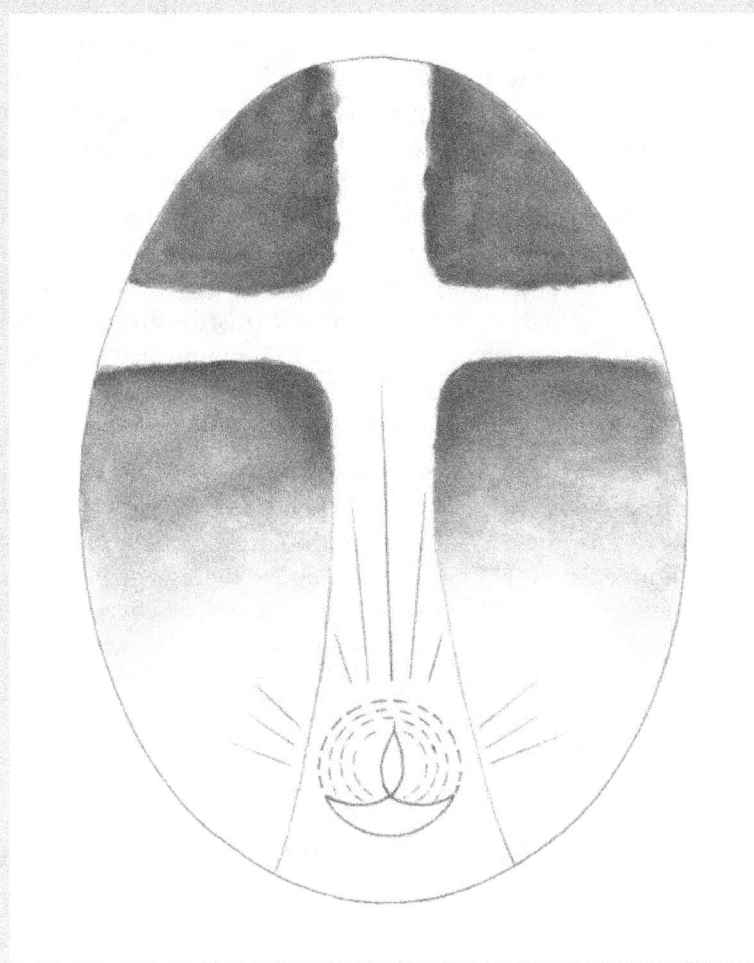

IX.1. The Human Suffering

Every religion communicates the message of God's saving presence: God is with us / within us as the God who loves us, heals us and leads us on the path of life to final liberation. Israel experienced the Divine as Yahweh: I am who am with you. In Jesus the disciples encountered the embodied presence of the Divine: Emmanuel, God with us. Hindus experience in Krishna the Bhagavan: the God who affectionately holds the devotee like a flute in his hands and awakens in it the divine melody. Muslims experience the Divine as Rahman, the compassionate God, who shows the path of salvation. For Buddhists the Buddha, the Enlightened One, is the way to nirvana. In every religion there is a basic experience that God is the saviour who encounters humans on the path of life and accompanies them to final integration. To surrender oneself totally to this God, who is our way and guide – this alone makes our life process free from worries and anxieties. This is faith; faith takes diverse forms; the diversity of these forms needs to be respected. "We need to have a great respect for everything that has been brought about in human beings by the Spirit that blows where it wills" (Pope John Paul II, Red. Miss. 56)

The first step on the way to salvation is honesty to oneself: humility to accept oneself with all the shadows and sinfulness, with all the sufferings and anxieties. Wrangling with suffering is a part of life; struggling with existential questions cannot be bypassed. The deepest agony of humans is loneliness: the feeling, *I have no one!* Even this has to be lived through. On the cross Jesus cried out: My God, my God, why have you forsaken me? (Mt. 27:46). With this Jesus went into the abysmal depth of human suffering: utter loneliness. There are agonising moments in our life, as we feel: God has forsaken me. When we are shaken to the foundations we cry out: why this suffering? This has to be honestly asked. And when asked, we realise that we need to live with a greater alertness to the divine Spirit that is ever present.

There are moments when we do not see the next step on our way: we do not know what to do or where to turn to. In such moments of the *dark night* it is important to become honestly aware of the inner movements, emotional as well as spiritual. Every crisis raises a challenge: look deep into your true self; every sickness has a message: change your way of life; every bit of loneliness is an invitation: surrender yourself to God in you. In such moments we realise: I cannot fall deeper than the divine ground from which I am born and through which I live. Every crisis when consciously encountered can become a kairos, an experience of intense grace.

> *Fear not,*
> *I am with you.*
> *Your grief will turn to joy*
>
> Jn. 16:20

> *Grieve not,*
> *I shall redeem you*
> *from all evils*
>
> Bh. Gita, 18: 66

Meditation

Posture: I sit straight, interiorly recollected. I come to a bodily silence.

Recollection: I look honestly into myself and take note of something that disturbs me deeply. I get in touch with the emotional movements in me: anxiety or fear, distress or despair, loneliness or guilt feeling. I let the doubts and questions surface in me. I allow the inner struggles with *my God* come to awareness. I ask *why* without expecting any immediate answer. I take myself in hand and confront the inner disturbances. I feel that I am walking on a dark path.

Inner word: *My God, my God, why have you forsaken me?* – I let this cry of Jesus be heard as the cry of the agony of my own soul. Or else, I dwell on the prayer: *I do not ask to see the distant scene – one step enough for me* (Newman).

IX.2. The Divine Suffering

We all have an inborn idea of God. With this we speak of God as the Almighty, the All-knowing and the All-pervading: Creator of everything and Lord of all. We imagine God as enthroned in glory in heaven, the God ever blissful, beyond all change and suffering.

With this beautiful image of God let us go up the hill of Calvary. There we stand before a man who hangs between heaven and earth – nowhere at home – crying out: My God, my God, why have you forsaken me! (Mt. 27:46). He could not come down from the cross for he was unable to *save himself*. (Mt. 27:42). With the eyes of faith we look deep into his tearful eyes, his bloodstained face and confess: this is God-with-us. When we do that all our inborn powerful symbols of God crumble and all the beautiful images of God turn into dust.

Here we are confronted with the paradox of faith in the crucified God:

- We conceive God as almighty, but the cross reveals to us a God who is weak and feeble (I Cor. 1:25).
- We imagine an all-knowing God, but the cross unfolds the foolishness of God (I Cor. 1:25).
- We look up to heaven in search of the transcendent God above history, but here God walks with us on the blood-stained paths of this earth.
- We conceive of a God who is enthroned above our heads as the Lord of all; but in Jesus God waits on us as a slave to wash our feet (Jn. 13:5).
- We imagine a God seated on the blissful peak of this universe, but in Jesus God meets us in this valley of tears.
- We often ask, why God does not intervene at the cruelties of human beings; but the cross shows how God himself has become a prey to human cruelty.

This is Emmanuel: God with us as the suffering God. This is the God who tells us: I am hungry, I am thirsty, I am homeless…(Mt. 25:35-36). God suffers with us because God loves us. To love means to respect the freedom of the other. Hence love makes one wounded. Only a vulnerable person can truly love; only a suffering God can be called *Love*. As long as there is so much poverty and sickness, sinfulness and suffering on this earth, we can only speak of a God who suffers with humanity.

This is portrayed in the parable of the wounded father (Lk. 15:11-32): till the return of the lost son, the father lived with a wounded heart. Till the eschatological moment when *God will be all in all,* God is a suffering God. The wound that is being laid in the heart of God through human sinfulness is laid open in the wounded heart of the crucified Lord. Jesus on the cross is the com*passiona*te face of God turned towards humanity.

> *The message of the Cross*
> *is foolishness;*
> *for us it is the power of God*
> I. Cor. 1:18.

> *From the self-immolation of the Creator*
> *the entire universe*
> *is born.*
> Rig Veda, 10. 90. 8-14

Meditation

Posture: I sit interiorly recollected and take note of a concrete situation of suffering either in my life or in the life of others: something that deeply distresses me.

Recollection: With trust and surrender I look intently on the face of the crucified Christ. If it is a help I keep a crucifix before me, or else I fix attention on the inner image of the crucified Lord. I let the form of the crucified God affect me deeply. I become intensely aware of God suffering with me / with others in this concrete situation. I try to feel the wounded love of God.

Inner word: In all seriousness I listen to the words of Christ addressed to me from the crucible of suffering: I am hungry...I am thirsty...I am homeless...

IX.3. The Healing Presence

Suffering and death cannot be the final end of life; if it were, life would have no meaning, and human creativity no hope to motivate. Something positive must evolve beyond suffering and death. The healing power and presence of the Divine is manifest in the risen Christ. The resurrection means that God has broken the devastating might of sin and suffering. The resurrection means that God has conquered the power of evil and the threat of death. This is an ongoing process of transformation. Our wounds are being healed and our estranged world is being reconciled to God. We are being delivered from slavery of the flesh to freedom in the Spirit (Rom. 8: 1-4). God walks with us on the blood-stained paths of this earth as a healing saviour. Faith in the risen Christ makes us say *yes* to life in spite of the destructive powers within and around us.

Love makes one vulnerable, but at the same time it enables one to remove the elements of suffering in the life of the beloved. Love re-creates what is destroyed and reassembles what is broken asunder. Love heals wounds and binds hearts together. Love enables one to forget the offence and forgive the other. Love opens our eyes to see the future brighter than the past. Love reaches out to infinite horizons. Love is creative: it recreates everything anew, ever new. Love transforms life. Love is a healing presence.

This healing power and presence of God's love has been made visible in the Resurrection of Christ. God is at work in our midst not only as participating in our suffering, but also as transforming our life into a new life. God's Spirit 'reconciles everything in and through Christ' towards the state when 'God will be all in all' (Col. 1: 20; 1Cor.15: 28). At the end of time everything will be transformed into the *body* of Christ; we will be filled with the utter *fullness of God* (Eph.3: 19). This eschatological state is prefigured in the risen Christ. This gives us unfailing hope.

We are called to take part in this divine work of cosmic reintegration. All our creative initiatives get thereby a divine horizon of meaning. Teachers enkindling light in the minds of students, nurses affectionately caring for the sick, social activists courageously bringing about justice and peace, farmers toiling hard to produce food, factory workers giving shape to things needed for a better living, artists unfolding the beauty of creation, scientists exploring the mysteries of reality… all those who are committed to shaping a more humane and just society take part in the divine work of reconciling this world to God. Human labour becomes participation in the resurrection of the cosmos to divine life. Faith in the risen Christ unfolds the sacred dimension of the secular.

> *The old is gone,*
> *see, everything has been made anew.*
>
> II. Cor. 5: 17

> *It is I who bring about*
> *harmony and welfare.*
>
> Bh. Gita, 9:22

Meditation

Posture: I sit straight interiorly recollected. I come to a bodily silence.

Breathing: I bring attention to breathing. I feel the stream of the pranah energy in the body. I try to feel how the divine stream of life refreshes my life. The breath of God breathes through me

Recollection: I recall a concrete realm of my work: something that I do for the good of others or for the transformation / preservation of nature. I feel into the divine dimension of this work. I understand that my work is participation in the divine work of bringing about peace and justice, healing and harmony. In it I perceive the Spirit of the risen Christ working through me. I am not the real subject of this work: God works through me. I am only an instrument in the reintegrating work of the Spirit. This makes me interiorly free.

Inner word: I dwell on: the work that I do is not my work, the divine Spirit works through me.

IX.4. The Divinisation

Who am I? – This is a basic question of spiritual life. Sages and mystics of all religions accompany the seekers in pursuing this question. This quest takes one to the deeper realms of self-understanding (*ātmabōdha*). Ultimately all spiritual paths point to the realization of the divine dimension of our being.

Christians have been given access to this inner realization through Jesus Christ. Through his life and teachings, through his death and resurrection, we are given the grace to realise that we are daughters / sons of God, heirs of God and coheirs of Christ. (Rom. 8:14-17). We are branches of the divine tree (Jn. 5:5), streams emerging from the divine fountain (Jn. 7:38), parts of the divine body (Rom. 12:5). The Spirit of the risen Christ streams through us and transforms our life into the divine life (Rom. 8:10-11). Christ is the true and ultimate subject of our being. In a moment of intense grace we may be able to cry out with Paul: "I live, not I, Christ lives in me" (Gal. 2:20). With it a mystical subject-consciousness evolves.

In the early Christian heritage this process is designated as *theosis*, divinization of the human. "Theosis means the re-forming of the Image of God according to which we have been created by the Word. The Word became man, so that we humans may become Divine." (Athanasius, De Incarnatione 3,101). "Through his immense love the Word of God became what we are, so that we may become perfectly what he is" (Iraeneus PG. 7,1120). "God became man, so that man may become God" (Augustine, PL. 38, 1997). "Christ takes shape in us through the Holy Spirit who reinstates the divinity in us." (Cyril of Alexandria, PG.75, 1088). "Through theosis we are brought into the energy-field of God." (Gregorios Palamas, Holy Hesychasts).

In Jesus Christ God became a human person in order to awaken the divinity inherent in us. In Christ we recognize the intimate union of the human with the Divine, the salvific reality that assures us that we too are called 'to be filled with the utter fullness of the Divine' (Eph. 3:19). Through Christ we have access to the realization that we are called to 'share the divine nature' (II. Pet. 1:4). Faith in Christ opens a divine horizon for our spiritual growth, an infinite depth for our spiritual consciousness (Eph. 4:13). This realization is a gift of divine grace, the work of the divine Spirit in us. Theosis is the experience of the deepest mystical union of the human with the Divine. Here we experience who we really are: *we are divine*! Here all genuine spiritual experiences converge. "The one who knows the Divine becomes divine" (*Brahmavid brahmaiva bhavati,* Mund. Up. 3.2.9). "The one who knows God becomes divine" (*Quisque Deum intelligit, deiformis fit*, Thomas Aquinas ST.I. 12.5.ad 3). "I am the God, whom I love" (Sufi Al-Hallaj).

> *You are called*
> *to share the divine nature*
> II. Peter 1:4

> *You are destined*
> *to become divine*
> Bh. Gita, 18:53

Meditation

Posture: I sit interiorly recollected and come to a deep bodily silence.

Breathing: With every breath I feel how the divine breath streams through me and the divine Spirit makes my body the temple of the Divine. (see Ex. II. 4)

Inner image: I take in the image of a tree and identify myself with a branch. I feel how the branch is being nourished and transformed by the inner flow of the vital sap. I am a branch on the divine tree constantly being enlivened and fructified by the stream of the divine Spirit. Or else, I take in the image of a fountain. I feel how the power of the stream is felt in every drop of water gushing out. I am like a drop on the divine fountain, constantly being energized by the divine Spirit. See Ex.V. 4, IV. 5)

Inner word: With the in-breath I feel the upward flow of pranah along the spinal cord, and with the out-breath I feel the pranah energy percolating the entire body. Then I repeat *sōham* (he I am). With every in-breath I say interiorly *sō*, and with the out-breath *ham*. After a while the word may recede into silence; I sit with a deep awareness of the divinisation process in me.

IX.5. The New Creation

Divinisation is a theonomous process taking place not only in humans but also in the entire universe. The divine light shines through all beings, and everything is being made transparent to the divine presence. In some way or other all religious traditions speak of this cosmic *theophany*. We breathe the breath of God (Job, 34:14). "See God in all things and all things in God" (Bh. Gita, 6: 30). The entire creation is awaiting the glory of God (Rom. 8:22).

Faith in the risen Christ opens our inner eye to the realization that the Spirit of Christ brings about a new creation. The entire reality was created in and through the divine Logos. (Jn. 1:1-5). Through the *Fall* an estrangement from the divine ground of being set in. Through the redemptive life and work of Jesus "God reconciled the estranged world to himself" (II. Cor. 5:18). Everything is being transformed to the dynamics of the Reign of God. This is a process that embraces the entire realm of creation. "The old is gone; everything is made new" (II Cor. 5:17). This is the work of the divine Spirit.

The resurrection of Christ reveals this cosmic immanence of the Spirit. It is not just an event of the past but the unfolding of the divine depth-dimension of the universe. The resurrection of Christ is the prefiguring and guarantee of a cosmic resurrection. In the risen Christ we recognize 'the first-born of the new creation' (I Cor. 15:23). "God wants all things to be reintegrated in and through Christ" (Col. 1:20) because 'in him, through him and unto him' all things have been created (Col. 1:16). Everything is being transformed into the body of Christ, since the entire creation has to attain its 'fullness in Christ' (Col. 1:19). In this all embracing spiritual process the presence of Christ vibrates in every atom and pulsates in every living cell. It is a Christophany: the presence of Christ shines through all.

This is however a painful process. In the entire creation one can feel the birth-pangs of the new creation. "From the beginning till now the entire creation has been groaning in one great act of giving birth. In these birth-pangs there is a hope of being freed from bondage to decadence, and being led into participation in the glorious freedom of the children of God. In this sense the entire creation is eagerly waiting for the revealing of the children of God" (Rom. 8:19-22). Through the suffering and agonies of reality – human as well as cosmic – a new creation is being born. We are called to participate in this dynamic evolution of the new creation in the power of the divine Sprit. Here spirituality gets a secular dimension; secular activities unfold a spiritual depth. Ultimately there is no gap between the sacred and the secular. The Incarnation of the divine Logos from within the womb of creation as well as the resurrection of Christ embracing the entire cosmos is the affirmation of the sacred significance of the secular.

At the end
God will be all in all
I Cor. 15: 28

Everything has to be
permeated by the divine Lord
Isa Up. 1.

Meditation

Posture: I walk on a quiet path, interiorly recollected, but united with all things around me.

Breathing: Through conscious breathing I feel the deep interconnectedness of all beings in the one flow of the pranah energy. I become gratefully aware of how the breath of God breathes through me and through all beings.

Recollection: I become aware of the power and presence of the divine Spirit that enlivens, nourishes and recreates everything. The presence of the Spirit permeates all like the vital sap of a tree streaming through the branches and leaves. I feel how fresh life unfolds all around me. I gratefully realise that I am part of this divine process.

Inner word: With every breath I repeat: *īśāvāsyamidam sarvam* (all this is permeated by the divine Lord, Isa Up. I).

10. The Now

Ultimately the spiritual journey leads to a deep mystical self-consciousness, to the realisation that *we are divine*. The concrete access to that is the ability to live in the present. The mind constantly takes us to the past or the future, the buddhi however enables us to stay in the present. Attentiveness to the movements of the divine Spirit in any given situation is the way to integral liberation. Eternity is the divine depth of the present moment

When asked what one should do in order to enter the Kingdom of God, Jesus did not give a list of things to do or rules to observe. He placed a child in their midst and said: be converted and become like a child (Mt. 18:3). The child lives fully in the present, at the given moment. 'Today, that is his name'. What enables entry to the Kingdom of heaven is the ability to feel into the divine depth of the *now* and relish the grace and respond to the demands of the Spirit here and now. Hence Jesus said: Learn from the birds of the air, from the lilies of the field; do not worry about tomorrow – live in today (Mt. 6:26-34)

In this series of meditations we are dwelling on some of the fruits of the spiritual process. The ability to live in the present presupposes inner freedom. Being freed from attachments one puts complete confidence in the divine master within. This means trust in oneself, confidence in the divine Self that unfolds through one's self. This in turn makes one transparent to the divine presence and creativity. One becomes constantly alert to the movements of the divine Spirit within oneself and all around. All this leads to a life of genuine compassion. Compassion is the hallmark of a person pursuing deep spirituality.

The Exercises:

1. I detach myself from the inner blocks within me: *off from me*
2. I put complete confidence in the divine master in me : *unto Thee*
3. I feel the utter transparency to the divine presence: *one with Thee*
4. I remain constantly attentive to the grace and demands of the Spirit: *new from Thee*
5. I feel how divine compassion streams forth through me.

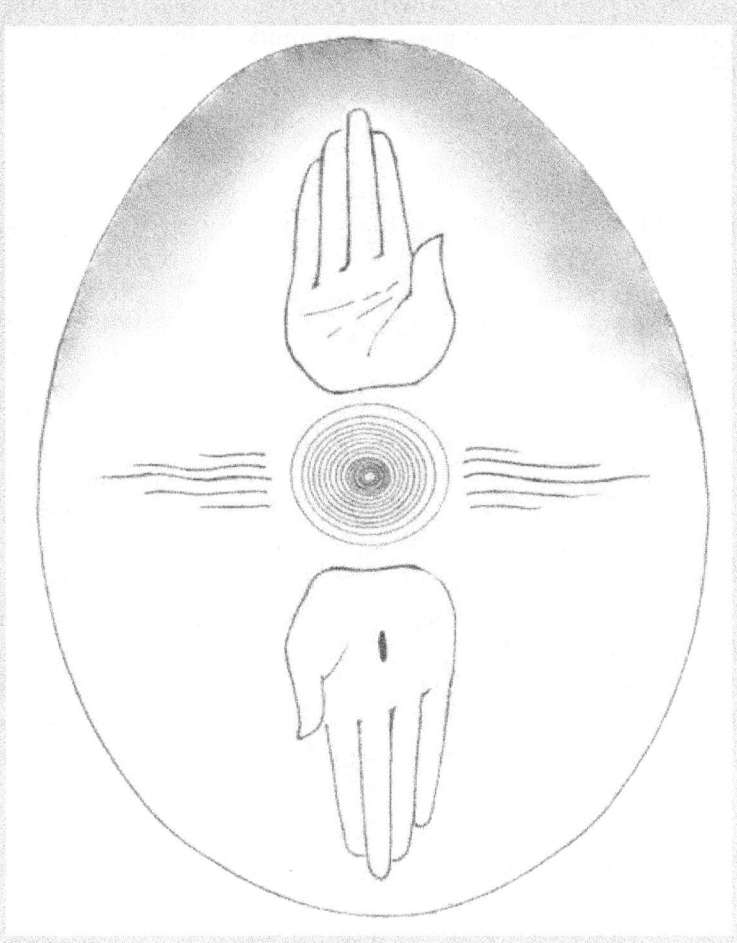

X.1. Inner Freedom

According to Indian sages and Christian mystics there are two centres of subject –consciousness: the ego and the self. The self works through the ego. But often at the ego-level the possessive nature of the mind can be so strong that the dominant ego-feeling gets uprooted from true self-consciousness. The result is a growing ego-fixation (*ahamkāra*). One gets bound to one´s greedy attachments and emotional interests. This makes the person unfree.

Growth in spiritual life means growth in genuine self-consciousness (*ātmabōdha*). It is the process of the realisation of one´s true self in relation to the divine Self within. This presupposes freedom from the grip of greed (*kāma*). What blocks the spiritual process of transformation is greed. One cannot serve two masters: God and greed, Jesus warned (Lk. 16:13). Greed is the primal cause of all suffering, Buddha said (Vinaya Pitaka). From greed evolves every form of estrangement (Bh. Gita, 2: 62-63).

How do we conquer greed? For this, spiritual masters of East and West demand asceticism. Without a basic ascetical attitude we cannot take a step forward in the spiritual life. True asceticism is not the negation of the sublime joys of the world or denial of the valid demands of the body. Asceticism is the attitude by which the sacredness of the world and of the body is respected. An ascetic perceives the world as the sacred sphere in which the Spirit integrates our life to divine life. An ascetic respects every human person as an expression of the Divine and looks at the things of nature as gifts of God meant for all. There is no place for manipulation of humans or exploitation of natural resources here. Asceticism is the matrix of love and joy, justice and harmony.

Concretely it demands a certain simplicity in life. One should be able to live happily with much less material possession. "Life does not become noble through what one owns" (Lk. 12:15). Consumerism is the modern slavery that makes people sick and frustrated. With much less possessions one is able to give more space to the divine Spirit within and all around oneself; and interpersonal relations too become more transparent. Asceticism means a counter-culture in today´s devastating consumer-culture. A healthy asceticism is the only effective antidote to the malaise of world capitalism that poisons the ethical marrow of human relationships and eats up the resources of the earth.

Asceticism demands discipline. Without discipline there is no growth in spiritual life. Discipline involves a certain regularity in spiritual exercises, consistency in decisions, truthfulness in relations and honesty to oneself. Discipline demands the courage to say *no* to certain things and the discernment to say *yes* to many others. Move with the inner movements of the divine Spirit – this is spiritual discipline. Asceticism makes one interiorly free, and discipline makes one alert to the Spirit.

> *If you hold on*
> *to your life,*
> *you lose it*
> Jn. 12:25

> *Renounce*
> *and enjoy.*
> Isa Up. 1.

Meditation

Posture: I go walking on a quiet path. I take every step slowly and consciously.

Breathing: I bring my attention to breathing and thereby I quieten my mind. I recall that every out-breath is a moment of death: a pre-experience of the last breathing out. With every out-breath I let myself go. I realise that ultimately I have nothing to hold on to. At some time I have to surrender everything that I possess, including my life-breath. With inner freedom I surrender myself to the divine Spirit, which breathes through me.

Recollection: I take every step consciously. With every new step I have to give up the foregoing step. I realise that only by giving up what I possess can I create space for the Spirit; only by breathing out do I make space for the in-breath. Trustfully abandoning the step behind and consciously breathing out I become deeply aware of the basic rhythm of life: let go and be open. I feel into myself and locate what blocks this process of letting go. I examine my attitudes to life and possessions, and discern the inner movement of the Spirit that motivates me to a life of asceticism and discipline, simplicity and inner freedom.

Inner word: At the beginning of every out-breath I say interiorly: *off from me.*

X.2. Confidence

As the sadhaka experiences inner freedom from the greedy ego-fixation confidence in the indwelling divine master grows; and *vice versa*. An intensive inter-personal relationship with God dwelling in us opens a tremendous scope for growth. It liberates the soul from its existential loneliness.

Take the case of a bird caught in a cage. It is ever restless: it flies in all possible directions but constantly hits on the rails. The bird is restless because it feels that it is created for the freedom beyond the cage. Hitting on the rail makes it feel that it is estranged from its true being; it feels the inability to overcome the loneliness. This image is often used to describe the existential loneliness of the human soul. Augustine expressed it succinctly: "Our heart is restless, Lord, until it finds rest in You" (Confessions. 1).

The deepest suffering of a human person is loneliness; and hence the deepest longing of the human soul is for divine Love, for the experience of a God who loves. As a personal *I* every human person is by nature oriented to a personal *thou*, ultimately to the divine *Thou*. There is an existential quest for a divine word of love in the stillness of the heart, for a divine ray of light in the dark night of the soul, for a divine touch of compassion in the moments of loneliness. Every religion tries to reveal this personal *face* of the Divine. Jews discover it in the covenant of Yahweh, Muslims find it in the Quranic revelation of Allah, Hindus experience it in the love of Krishna, and Buddhists find it in the enlightened path of the Buddha. Christians have encountered the compassionate face of God turned towards humanity in Jesus the Christ. But these forms of the divine self-revelation are not to be just fixed on an event or a person of the past; rather they manifest the God within us / God with us in the present. God meets us here and now, from within our heart, in the midst of the complexities of life. Christ is God-with-us in the divine depth of the *now*.

Such an intimate encounter evokes confidence. With great confidence one can surrender oneself to God in the heart. It is ultimately the surrender of the human soul to the divine spouse, the let-go of the true human self into the divine Self within. When one lets oneself unconditionally fall into the divine ground of being, existential anxiety is conquered and loneliness is overcome.

Confidence evokes trust; trust renders a sense of security, which in turn gives rise to the *courage to be* and a joyous self-esteem. The experience of being loved by the divine Lord accompanies the sadhaka as a liberating force. "If you are led by the Spirit, you are free, for Christ has made you free" (Gal. 5:1, 18). "If you trust in me, you shall overcome all hurdles" (Bh. Gita, 18: 58).

> *The one who follows me,*
> *shall not walk in darkness,*
> *but have the light of life*
> Jn. 8:12

> *To the one who worships me*
> *with love*
> *I give the grace of*
> *inner integration*
> *and access to me*
> Bh. Gita, 10:10

Meditation

Posture: I go walking on a quiet path. I take every step slowly and consciously.

Breathing: I bring attention to breathing and thereby I quieten my mind.

Recollection: I become aware of my deep quest for divine guidance, for divine light, for a divine master, who accompanies me. I gratefully recall a moment of intense closeness to the Lord in my life.

Inner image: I feel that Christ the divine master walks with me on my path. He meets me from within the heart. Trusting in him I take every step with him consciously and joyfully.

Inner word: Towards the end of every out-breath I say interiorly: *unto Thee.*

X.3. Transparency

Freedom from bondage to the ego-fixation and confidence in the inner divine master gradually evolve into the experience of total transparency to the divine presence within. The inter-personal relationship with the divine master matures in the transpersonal experience of transparency to the divine ground of being. Encounter with the divine thou gets deepened into a mystical oneness with the divine Self. Word merges into silence, love attains union. Active life then evolves out of the divine centre, through it and in it.

Mystics of all religions ultimately accompany the seekers to this experience of oneness. They use poetic symbols to describe this intimate experience: as a river flowing into the ocean (Upanishads), as a drop of rain-water merging into the sea (Teresa of Avila), as a prism fully letting the sunlight beam through it (John of the Cross), as a flame is one with the fire (Meister Eckhart), as a piece of iron glows in fire (Rumi). The individuality of the human soul is not annihilated, but transformed into life in the divine Spirit. The human consciousness is made translucent to the divine Light. The human is made utterly transparent to the Divine. God shines through me. I become one with the Divine. In the deepest mystical experience one exclaims: *I am divine!*

Jesus experienced this divine breakthrough in his consciousness. "I am in the Father, the Father is in me: we are One" And to this mystical consciousness he invites all who believe in him. (Jn. 17:21-22). Our life evolves in Christ, in God, within the inner-trinitarian process of life. Christ is the reality of our deepest oneness with the Divine in the depth of the *eternal now*.

This transparency to the Divine within us is a work of the Spirit in us; it is a gift of grace. Our consciousness is deepened through the breakthrough of the divine light. This enlightenment experience is bound with inner joy. It is the bliss that comes from inner freedom and transparency. Indian sages speak of bliss (*ananda*) as the fruit of the mystical union (Bh. Gita, 6: 20-21). Paul describes peace and joy as fruits of the divine Spirit (Gal. 5: 22). Jesus promised his disciples participation in the divine glory that shone through him (Jn. 17:24). A person who goes through the spiritual process of inner transformation will emerge as a joyous person. Real joy comes from the realisation that God is the true subject of one´s life and work.

They are in me,
I am in them
Bh. Gita, 9:29

Father, just as you are in me,
and I am in you,
may they all be one in us,
fully one.
Jn. 17:21, 23

Meditation

Posture: I go walking on a quiet path. I take every step slowly and consciously.

Breathing: I bring attention to breathing and thereby I quieten my mind. While breathing in I feel the upward flow of the pranah energy along the spinal cord, and while breathing out I feel the downward flow into the whole body. I feel further how the pranah energy streams forth beyond me through all beings.

Recollection: I become aware of the deep oneness with all beings: all are bound together in the one divine stream of life and love. I sense how divine Life percolates through all beings. With inner joy I feel the transparency of my being to the divine presence

Inner image: I imagine myself to be a prism through which the divine light passes through, or a branch of the divine tree whose vital sap, the Spirit, streams through me.

Inner word: As every out-breath comes to an end, there is a pause for a moment. In the stillness of this pause I say interiorly: *one with Thee.*

X.4. Attentiveness

Transparency to divine presence, oneness with the divine ground of being, enables the sadhaka to live with attentiveness: one is attentive to the grace and demands of the divine Spirit here and now. To be attentive means to be totally present to the present moment. In fact, what I *have* is only the present moment. The past is gone; the future is not yet in my hands. What I truly possess is a fraction of a second. What I do have is the present breath; whether I can breathe in again is not certain. Life evolves not so much from the past to the future, but from the *present* to the *present*. Spiritual discipline would make one deeply sensitive to the present moment.

Attentiveness to the present moment means alertness to the dynamics of the divine Spirit within me and all around. Attentiveness is listening to what the Spirit is saying to me here and now. Eternity as total transparency to the Divine unfolds from within the divine depth of the *now*. If we can, enlightened by divine grace, look deep into the inner sacred space, we perceive the *heavens* in us. There God dwells, and from there the Spirit transforms our life. There we touch eternity. Referring to this 'eternal now' (*nunc aeternum*) Jesus said: "On that day you will realise that you are in me and I in you; the one who hears my word and believes in him who sent me, *has* eternal life; he *has passed* from death to life" (Jn. 14:20; 5:24). Jesus invites us to a deeper consciousness.

Attentiveness makes one fully alive. One is able to pay full attention to what one is engaged in and full respect to the person one meets here and now. Attentiveness overcomes distractions, keeps the mind focussed, regulates emotional movements and deepens awareness. It conquers fatigue and strengthens concentration. It gives colours to our relationships and imagination to our commitment. Deeply grounded in the present one takes wings towards the wide horizons of service and creativity.

Attentiveness makes one sensitive to the 'Spirit that blows where it wills' (Jn. 3, 8). It enables the seeker to have a genuine respect for the diverse ways in which the divine Spirit is working in the hearts of people, in cultures and religions. With the inner *divine eye* one can capture the vibrations of the divine Word in the Scriptures of religions, the transforming power of the divine Spirit in their symbols, the channels of divine grace in their rituals, the evolution of the Reign of

God in their ennobling values. When we are attentive to the Spirit we respect followers of other religions as co-pilgrims, guided by the one Spirit and led to the one final goal. Attentiveness makes one 'worship God in Spirit and Truth'. (Jn, 4, 24). What God demands is not compulsive religiosity, but spiritual sensitivity to the grace and demands of the Divine in the *now*.

> *Stay attentive;*
> *stand alert.*
> Mt. 24:42, 44

> *The one who is attentive*
> *attains inner wisdom*
> *and reaches ultimate peace.*
> Bh. Gita, 4: 39

Meditation

Posture: I go walking on a quiet path. I take every step slowly and consciously.

Breathing: I breathe in and out consciously and relaxed. I remain fully attentive to every in-breath and out-breath.

Recollection: I remain recollected on one thought: *the breath of God breathes through me.* I do not let any other thought come in. I stay attentive to the life-giving movement of the Spirit in me. I remain fully present to the present moment.

Inner image: With every in-breath I feel how the energy of the divine breath flows into me and gives me a new birth.

Inner image: With every in-breath I say interiorly: *new from Thee.*

X.5. Compassion

Spirituality is the experience of the Spirit: deep within and all around. Through meditative pursuits the consciousness is deepened and one perceives the divine Spirit within the inner sacred space. With this *insight* one looks into the world and perceives the same divine Spirit active all around. In a two-fold experience all spiritual paths meet: the realisation that we are divine, and the perception of God in all, all in God. Ultimately it is the experience of the Spirit transforming the entire reality to a new creation, to participation in divine life. God is with us (*Emmanuel*) as the God who suffers with us and transforms our life.

We humans experience this presence of the Divine in our midst, and communicate this experience to one another through compassion. In it there is an element of suffering with the other (*cum-passio*), journeying with the other. It is not just a matter of an emotional response. Genuine compassion emerges from within the sacred space of the person. The love of the indwelling Spirit flows out as compassion. Hence through the channel of compassion we communicate divine love to one another. God is the actual source and subject of compassion. Compassion has a mystical as well as a prophetic dimension. Compassion evokes critique on inhuman structures and values. Compassion makes one courageous to protest against injustice. Compassion leads to solidarity.

In all religions compassion is extolled as the hallmark of a truly spiritual person, as the primary path to liberation. "Be friendly and compassionate towards all beings" (Hinduism, Bh. Gita, 12: 13). "Compassion is the essential Buddha nature hidden in all" (Buddhism, Mahaparinirvana Sutta, 259). "Compassion alone ennobles life" (Jainism, Panchastikaya 137). "Where compassion vanishes, humanness disappears" (Taoism, Chaunachu, 23). "God wants compassion, not ritual sacrifices" (Judaism, Hosea, 6:6). "More valuable than prayer is compassion" (Islam, Quran, 2: 177). All religions point to God as the Compassionate One; humans attain God through compassion.

Jesus was a compassionate person. In his dealings with the poor and the marginalised, the sick and the lonely, the women and the children, Jesus was an embodiment of divine compassion. In him we recognise the compassionate face of God turned towards humanity. "Blessed are the compassionate!" – Jesus proclaimed (Mt. 5:7). Over against the prevalent religiosity of ritualism and legalism Jesus upheld compassion as the way to God (Mk. 12:33, Mt. 5:23, Lk. 11:42). The parables of the compassionate Samaritan (Lk. 10:29-37) and of the merciful father (Lk. 15:11-32) show that God wants compassion, not so much ritual practices or legal observances (Mt. 9:13). Compassion is the fruit of contemplation.

> *Be compassionate*
> *just as God is compassionate*
> Lk. 6:36

> *Be compassionate*
> *towards all beings.*
> Bh.. Gita, 12: 13

Meditation

Posture: I go walking on a quiet path. I take every step slowly and consciously.

Breathing: I breathe in and out consciously feeling the divine presence deep within me and all around.

Recollection: I sense the divine presence in all things, in all persons, especially in the poor and the sick.

Inner image: I recall to mind the image of a suffering person; I look deep on to his / her face and perceive the divine presence there.

Inner word: with every breath I repeat: *be compassionate.*

Silence Empowers Us

A genuine seeker was exploring the enlightening power of silence for several years in an ashram. He came to no enlightenment. One day he approached the Master and asked:

"What more can I do to achieve enlightenment?"

"So very little," – the Master answered, "just as you cannot do anything to make the sun rise tomorrow".

That disappointed the disciple. "Why then should I pursue this hard discipline of the daily exercise of silence?" he asked.

"So that you may not sleep, when the sun rises!", was the reply of the Master.

Be alert – this is the power of silence.

Keep awake! – this is the call of meditation.

A growing sensitivity to the inner movements of the divine Spirit – this is the fruit of spiritual discipline.

Meditation is a receptive process to listen to the Spirit, not a hectic activity to conquer God-experience.

"If you know God, it is not God!" (St. Augustine)

In silence consciousness sinks from mental objectification through meditation towards the intuitive awareness in contemplation, and further it expands to the perception of the Divine in all beings.

In silence there is a delving into contemplation and surfacing in compassion.

This is a process that demands human asceticism and discipline; but it evolves in the power of divine grace and light.

Deep in the ocean a little fish asked a big fish: "Where is the ocean?"

The big fish replied: "You, little one, you are swimming in the ocean; realise that!"

The little fish was not satisfied with this answer. It went on asking every one: "Where is the ocean?"

Silence helps us to know that 'we live and move and have our being' in the divine ocean.

Silence makes us experience the Divine as the ultimate *subject* of our life: the inner ground and fountain, the inner light and life.

Silence empowers us to realise that we are branches of the divine tree, channels of the divine fountain, waves of the divine ocean, flames of the divine fire.

Know, who you are; become, what you are:

You are divine!

Appendix:

Body as the Language of Prayer
A Meditative Form of Sūryanamaskar
(Sun Salutation)

We are bodily beings. Body is the primordial language of humans. Body is the first place of meeting the Divine. If God came to us through the body we have to go to God in and through the body. Experiencing the body as the *temple* of the divine Spirit is the basis of spirituality. It is through the body that we wake to the transforming presence of the Spirit in and around us.

A simple but effective way to this primal experience is the daily morning practice of Sūryanamaskar. It is not an exercise of worshipping the sun, but greeting the rising sun as the symbol of the divine Light that breaks anew into our life every day. More than that, it is a way of awakening the divine Sun within us: sensing the divine Life and Light within the inner sacred space.

In the classical yoga form Sūryanamaskar is practiced with the rhythm of breathing. Here I am proposing a meditative form of this exercise: stay for a moment at every posture and feel into oneself, into the body, mind and heart. Just be here and now: be present to the present moment. At the divine depth of the *now* become aware of the inner movements of the Spirit.

Take for instance the posture of standing with extended hands looking into the sunlight. Feel the form of the body at this moment and sense the utter openness that the body language communicates. Feel into the mind and sense how happy you will be when you are genuinely open to persons and things today. Feel into the inner sacred space and become aware of the grace of love and joy that your transparence to the Spirit brings about.

How long should one stay at a posture? – this is left to each one. Less than a minute would suffice. The duration may vary from posture to posture depending on the inner attentiveness. One need not aspire to take every posture in the perfect form demanded in the classical yoga-āsanas. One could rather be flexible with regard to the movements of the body. It is important that the entire exercise evolves in a flowing way, one posture merging into the next.

The main concern is awareness: to be present to the present moment. The body is always in the present; it is the mind that constantly takes us to the past and future. During the day we are constantly steered by the mind. Our family and profession force us always to think ahead, to plan and move on. Inevitably we tend to live into the future. Or, we get bogged down by the elements and experiences of the past. We are hardly in the present. But what we have is only the present, a fraction of a second; the past is gone, the future is not here. Still we tend to live either in the past or in the future! This makes our mind tired and our body exhausted. Before we start the hectic day, we shall take a few minutes to stay consciously in the body: to become aware of the power of the *now*. We take it as a sacred time, to be present to the present moment. Gradually we realise that the hidden divine well-springs evolve into a living fountain that waters our daily life.

Twenty postures are proposed in this exercise. Most of the postures are in tune with the classical form of Sūryanamaskar. A few are inserted to add to the meditative quality of the exercise. For each posture the following elements are given: (a) the meaning in a word (b) the practical guidelines for the posture (c) a formula that evokes the awareness (d) a relevant text each from Christian and Hindu Scriptures. These are only helps for the beginners. After some weeks of regular practice each one should be able to sense for oneself the meaning of the posture and message of the body. Gradually each person could develop one's own meditative form of the Sūryanamaskar according to the inner movements of the Spirit and demands of life.

This daily exercise of deepening the awareness in a bodily way would add a spiritual quality to one's daily life. One is enabled to live the day more consciously: to be more present to persons and attentive to duties. An abiding sense of the divine presence pervades the day.

1. Rootedness

- Close your eyes.
- Stand straight, relaxed and firm.
- Imagine yourself as a tree and feel being rooted in the earth.

Rooted in the divine ground I will live this day.

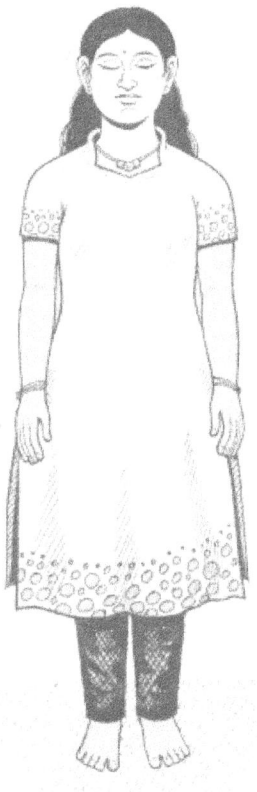

I am formed out of the earth (Gen. 2:7)
My body is earth waking to consciousness (Chand. Up. 3. 12. 3)

2. Presence

- Slowly bring the hands folded at the heart-centre (*Anjali*)
- Feel lovingly through the whole body and sense the enlivening power of the breath.
- Feel the heart-beat and be grateful that the last night was not your very last night.

   I am thankful for being here, thankful for this new day.

My body is the temple of the divine Spirit (I Cor. 6:19)

My body is the temple wherein divine consciousness abides (Bh. Gita, 13: 2)

3. Transparence

- Open slowly the palms at the heart-centre, opening yourself.
- Feel into the hands and sense the utter openness

I am like an open vessel: ready to give, ready to receive.

God is Spirit: all who worship God must worship Him in Spirit and Truth (Jn. 4:24)

OM, fullness there, fullness here, fullness comes forth from fullness, take fullness from fullness, fullness remains (Brih. Up. 5. 1)

4. Openness

- Extend the arms fully, pening yourself totally.
- For the first time look consciously into the daylight and feel gratefully the sunbeams brightening up your day
- Sense the openness in body, mind and heart, total openness to the divine Spirit.

This day is a grace and a call. Joyfully I welcome the sun of this new day.

Whoever does the truth, comes out into the light (Jn. 3:21)

From the unreal lead me to the Real, from darkness lead me to Light, from death lead me to Immortality (Brih. Up. 1. 3. 28) .

5. Joy

- Move the hands upward closing in above the head like a lotus-bud
- Look upward and open the hands like a lotus-flower
- Feel how the energy of the sun penetrates your body and awakens within you the power of the earth

In the divine sun my life grows and blossoms joyfully.

Trust in the Light in order to become a child of Light (Jn.12:36)

The Light beyond the heavens is the same Light that shines within the heart (Chand. Up. 3. 13. 7).

6. Service

- Stretch yourself a bit backwards; then slowly bend forward.
- Bring your hands to your knees, or further below, and stay bent forward.

Liberated from fear I am fully here, ready to serve.

If I have washed your feet, you must wash each others´ feet (Jn. 13:14)

Work with inner freedom for the welfare of the world (Bh. Gita, 3:25)

7. Trust

- Bend down further, fix the hands on the floor, stretch back the right leg; keep the back straight.
- Look ahead into the sunlight.

Full of trust and confidence I set out on my way.

Go on your way while you have the Light (Jn. 12:35)

With an enlightened mind, free from greed, work for the good of all beings (Bh. Gita, 4: 23).

8. Let Go

- Stretch back both the legs and slowly lie down on the stomach and stretch your hands forward.
- The entire body remains relaxed on the ground
- Gratefully feel: my body and the earth are one.

I cannot fall deeper than to the divine ground which always bears me.

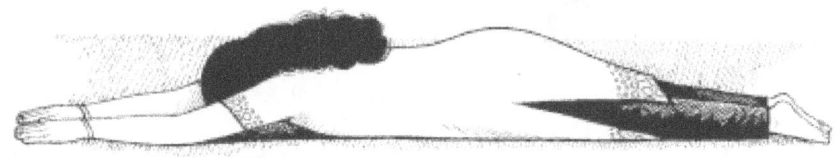

The grain of wheat has to fall on the earth and die, so that it yields a rich harvest (Jn. 12:24).

Renounce and enjoy! (Isa Up. 1)

9. Hope

- Raise the head and the upper part of the body, steady yourself with the arms on the floor and look into the daylight again.
- Joyfully take in the enlivening warmth of the sun into your body.

Out of the divine ground I live my life with trust and hope.

God has called us out of the darkness into his wonderful Light (I Pet. 2:9)

Everything shines after his Light; it is his Light that illumines everything (Mund. Up. 2. 2. 11).

10. Love

- Lift the knees and bend the body to an arch position.
- Feel the anchoring in your hands and feet.

Like a bridge I bind people together.

When we love one another, we are in God and God dwells in us (I Jn. 4:12)

Walk together, speak with one another, may your minds be united, and your hearts bound in love (Rig Veda, 10. 191. 2-4).

11. Respect

- Slowly sit back on the heels and bend forward; let the forehead touch the earth. The hands rest on the ground.
- Feel gratefully the nourishing power of the mother earth.

I bow before creation with reverence..

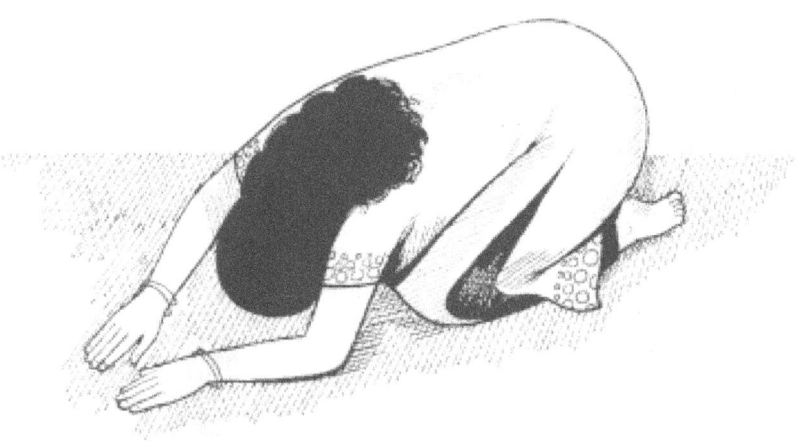

Everything has been created in and through the Word, which is the inner Life and the Light (Jn. 1:1-5).

God dwells in the hearts of all things; they are all being moved by his energy (Bh. Gita, 18:61)

12. Stillness

- Sit straight and keep the palms laid open on the knees.
- Keep your eyes closed and listen to the inner divine voice.

I want to be attentive to listen to the divine voice among the many voices.

Whoever comes from God, listens to the Word of God (Jn. 8:47).

I am your disciple, I take refuge in you, teach me, Lord (Bh. Gita, 2:7).

13. Courage

- Fix the hands on the floor, stretch back the left foot and look ahead
- Keep the back straight
- Look into the sunlight.

Full of confidence I look forward to the new day daring new steps.

I forget what lies behind me; I strain forward to what awaits me in front (Phil. 3:13).

Take refuge in me; I shall liberate you from all your sufferings; grieve not (Bh. Gita, 18:66).

14. Awareness

- Straighten up the body slowly; let the hands slide over the body upward.
- Occasionally stop and feel the respective part of the body, eg. abdomen, heart, face
- Feel through the body with love and gratitude

I live this day fully with alertness to my vital energies, my emotions, my speech, my listening, my thinking…

Whatever you eat or drink, whatever you do, do it all for the glory of God (I Cor. 10:31).

Whatever you eat, whatever you do, whatever you offer, do it all as an offering to the Lord (Bh. Gita, 9:27)

15. Alertness

- Move the hands over the face and bring them folded in between the two eye-brows.
- Stay for a while and feel the center of your mental power.

May the divine light shine through me and transform me.

When your whole body is filled with Light, it will be entirely bright, as when a lamp shines through you (Lk. 11:36).

God is the Light dwelling in the hearts of all (Bh. Gita, 13:18).

16. Light

- Raise the folded hands upward above the head and stand like a burning lamp; keep the eyes closed.
- Feel in the body the warmth ascending along your spine.

May I be a light that kindles other lights.

You are the light of the world, a light that has to shine before others (Mt. 5:14, 16).

May the Light shine through my body; may I become a bearer of immortality (Tait. Up. 1, 4).

17. Blessing

- Take slowly the hands apart and extend the arms in blessing, with the palms opened downward.
- Think of the persons you will meet today and send them vibrations of blessing

Let me be a blessing for the people around me.

Blessed are the compassionate, they shall have compassion shown to them (Mt. 5:7).

The one who is friendly and compassionate to others is dear to me (Bh. Gita, 12:13).

18. Peace

- With the hands stretched out let the upper part of the body turn in all four directions.
- Greet the environment and the whole creation and send vibrations of peace to all.

Let me bring peace wherever I go.

Blessed are those who promote peace, they shall be called daughters and sons of God (Mt. 5:9).

May all beings attain peace and harmony, welfare and happiness (ancient Indian blessing).

19. I am

- Bring the hands back to the heart-centre and keep them folded
- Bowing forward greet the entire reality with a smile of joy and love.

Namaste! The Divine in me greets the Divine in you!

The Kingdom of God is within you (Lk. 17:21).

May we seek divine Light together (Katha Up, 1, 1).

20. Meditation

- Sit straight and relaxed. Sink into a deep meditative silence.
- Be present to the present moment
- Wake to the awareness of the divine presence within and all around, especially in the encounters and events of this day

Who am I?

Go to the inner silent space, meet the Divine therein (Mt. 6:6).

Seek the Divine within the silent space in you (Chand. Up. 8.1.1).

www.ingramcontent.com/pod-product-compliance
Lightning Source LLC
Chambersburg PA
CBHW080919170426

43201CB00016B/2202